Design
Democracy

Copyright © 2025 by William Robertson
All rights reserved.

No part of this book may be reproduced, stored in a retrieval system, or transmitted in any form or by any means: electronic, mechanical, photocopying, recording, or otherwise without prior written permission of the publisher, except for brief quotations used in reviews, articles, or scholarly analysis.

Title: *Design Democracy: The Death and Life of the Human Workplace*
Author: William Robertson
Publisher: Design Build Labs

ISBN Hardback: 979-8-9939842-0-9
ISBN E-book: 979-8-9939842-1-6
ISBN Paperback: 979-8-9939842-2-3

Printed in the United States of America.

First Edition

Design Democracy

The Death and Life of the Human Workplace

William Robertson

Thank you Amanda, Summer and Sienna. It's all for you.

*"We don't rise to the level of our expectations,
we fall to the level of our training."*
— *Archilochus*

Contents

Preface xi
Introduction 1

Chapter 1: Confronting Fear - Finding Dragons 5
Chapter 2: Enterprise-Level Empathy -
        The Architect and the Ghost 13
Chapter 3: The Stardust of Innovation 23
Chapter 4: The Missing Voice in Design 39
Chapter 5: Transactional Design 49
Chapter 6: Patterns of Life 59
Chapter 7: Culture Over Tradition 71
Chapter 8: Design for Real Life 81
Chapter 9: Dream Teams 91
Chapter 10: Consensus, Compromise, and Truth 103
Chapter 11: Courage to Innovate 115
Chapter 12: Visibly Valuable 123
Chapter 13: Endurance & Iterations 135
Chapter 14: Tough Empathy 145
Chapter 15: Completing the Circle 157
Chapter 16: The Architecture of Courage 165

Appendix A: Case Studies 169
    Case Study 1: A Cautionary Tale of Design Privilege 169

Case Study 2: The Power of Listening 173
Case Study 3: The "We'll Take It from Here" Fallacy 177
Case Study 4: The High Cost of a Low Price 181
Case Study 5: The Indisputable Project Record 185
Case Study 6: The $250,000 Slow Win 189
Appendix B: The Design Democracy Playbook 193
Appendix C: A Brief History of Empathy
       The Cornerstone of Design Democracy 199
Appendix D: Survey Examples 203
Acknowledgements 205
Index 207

Preface

"What do you want to be when you grow up?"
By age three I had my answer.

"Architect," I told anyone willing to listen. I don't know where it came from. No one in my family was an architect. I didn't know any architects growing up, but it's been calling to me since the time I could speak.

Whenever I could get it, I found work in design and construction. My very first job was pushing a broom on a jobsite for a local general contractor in Massachusetts. I was twelve. When I wasn't pushing puddles of water into a sump pump for hours in a dark, musty basement I moved piles of lumber from one place to another, one sheet of plywood at a time. This internship of hard knocks continued summer after summer, through middle school, high school, and college, as I grew from laborer to carpenter.

It wasn't a fast-track to greatness, but I knew I was on the right path. Collaborative design was calling to me, but my vision for it was still hazy. What I felt most clearly was a deep sense of disconnection, a feeling that began on construction sites in my teens and followed me into architecture offices. Idea formation, design, and construction felt like separate, warring kingdoms, each operating in a vacuum. The most glaring casualty of this siloed process was the end-user; time and again, the final product seemed to ignore their most basic needs. But whenever I asked why, on the jobsite or the drafting room floor, I was met with a shrug. It was my first encounter with the invisible wall of design privilege, the unspoken rule that such questions were not to be asked. I could see I'd have to build a new system from scratch, and that I'd have to break things in the process. So that's what I did.

I fought with teachers, professors, and advisors; I was sure I knew better. In retrospect, I wish I had suppressed my combative ideas and listened to their teaching so I could better explain how and why I wanted to break the established rules. But I didn't do it that way. I was set on designing my own life and everything in its path.

I entered Cornell University's College of Architecture, Art, and Planning in the fall of 1993. From the very beginning, I took an unconventional path, sensing that the standard blueprint for an architect was missing something essential. Instead of the typical 5-year professional degree, a rigid track that left little room for outside perspective, I chose to build my own curriculum from figure drawing, painting, art history, and English literature. This path was a direct challenge to the design privilege embedded in the traditional system, which seemed to value technical proficiency over a deep, humanistic understanding. I was sure that to create spaces for people, I first needed to learn about people, their stories, their history, and their art. This combination would go on to serve me well, but back then it meant nothing on paper, greatly complicating my career prospects and delaying my licensure process. I could have done this a little differently too, but I didn't.

I applied to positions I was underqualified for. I started companies long before I should have. I fought with my supervisors. I argued with the people who were paying me. I sent the emails you shouldn't send. I fired my clients.

And somehow, despite all this, or perhaps because of it, I became a top-performing strategist for three of the most sought-after real estate consulting firms in the world. I waged a daily war against the industry's entrenched design privilege. My methods weren't always graceful, but they were a direct challenge to the status quo. I insisted that my role wasn't just to manage a schedule and budget, but to practice an early form of Enterprise-Level Empathy—to advocate for the hundreds of people who would actually use these spaces. Brokers would flinch when I'd overstep their sales script, but it turns out that a process rooted in broader listening was what everyone wanted but didn't know how to ask for. The data was our first proof of concept for a "Predictive Placemaking" strategy; the teams I supported were winning more, and my department outperformed similar groups globally 3-to-1. The early days of Design Democracy were a success.

But I was winning the battles while losing the war. I was burning bridges everywhere. My raw form of Tough Empathy was alienating the very people I needed to convince; anyone who didn't do it my way, I either fought with or ghosted. This led to some essential questions. Was my own fear of failure making me needlessly aggressive? Could I build a revolution without starting a war in every meeting? I had proven the *what* and the *why* of this new approach, but I had to find a more sustainable, more truly empathetic *how*.

My first step toward this goal was to get better at listening, both to myself and others. I knew it was important to get good at seeing the signal in the noise. Large-scale, data-driven listening is a superpower, but the antidote to my confrontational approach needed to be stronger than that. I needed to pair listening with a deeper understanding of what others were saying to truly create empathy. That's what I really needed. Empathy with individuals and empathy with small, medium, and large groups of colleagues, clients, and peers. I realized that seeing the answer in a dataset wasn't enough; I needed to be using the information I gleaned from empathetic listening to do better things for real people and their environment.

Empathy, I learned, requires all of us to get comfortable with getting a little uncomfortable.

Easier said than done.

I couldn't just decide one day that I was going to empathize more with people and their teams. I had to work for it. How was I going to walk a mile in their shoes, I wondered—so many people, so many miles.

Then I was starting a company again. This time, though, my business formula and my new operating philosophy worked. I paired the humble business development efforts of this new company with life changes that would allow me to conquer the fears that had previously prevented peaceful business relationships. I was on a new journey, one where I challenged myself to better empathize with the challenges of my colleagues and clients.

In these pages, I share the stories of this journey. Some stories emerge from my successes and failures in commercial architecture. Some stories come from the harrowing physical challenges that eroded my ideas of privilege and propelled me toward the empathy that's at the core of Design Democracy.

I knew I needed to confront my own fears before I could ask everyone else to confront theirs. I am far better at feeling people's pain points because I am now more comfortable getting uncomfortable. I now know that it's good for me to expose myself to a little pain so that I can more deeply understand pain. I still work with clients who don't understand the need to get uncomfortable, the need to face the real truths, but the ones who do get more out of the Design Democracy process.

Revolutionizing the collaborative design process, the core of this book, depends on overcoming personal fears of all kinds; chief among them, the fear of the unfamiliar. Every story I've included addresses that theme. The journey of design and the journey of life work together, and by embracing the unfamiliar, shedding our privilege, and confronting our fears, anyone can develop the empathy needed to nourish a Design Democracy.

Let's get just a little uncomfortable together.

Introduction

Our buildings are failing us. We invest billions of dollars in constructing the hospitals, schools, and headquarters that shape our lives, yet they are often dysfunctional, uninspiring, and profoundly disconnected from the needs of the people inside them. Walk into any generic corporate office, and you'll feel it instantly: the sterile lighting, the maze of soulless cubicles, the conference rooms that feel more like interrogation chambers. These are not just aesthetic failures; they are human failures. These soulless spaces create friction, drain energy, and stifle the very creativity and collaboration they are meant to foster.

This is not a failure of budget or materials; it is a failure of empathy. It is the direct result of design privilege, a broken, top-down process where a select few make decisions based on ego, outdated assumptions, and a profound insulation from real-world consequences. This privilege manifests in a C-suite approving a design that reflects their personal tastes but ignores the daily workflow of hundreds of employees. This design privilege lives in the architect who designs for that stunning photo feature in a magazine, not for the messy realities of human interaction. This broken system is propped up by traditional methods like focus groups, which have become Petri dishes for *preference falsification*: the phenomenon where people misrepresent their true desires to conform to perceived social pressures. The result of this is a massive gamble, a multimillion-dollar bet on an outcome that is almost guaranteed to be flawed because it was based on bad data from the start. This book is a declaration of war on that privilege. It is a playbook for a quiet revolution.

That revolution is Design Democracy, a leadership philosophy designed to systematically generate Enterprise-Level Empathy. It is a structured, data-driven methodology that provides a framework for leaders to make authentic, courageous decisions through a series of consensus-building tools and surveys. The process, however, is not for the faint of heart. It requires that business leaders and designers intentionally confront fear. The fear of losing control, the fear of consensus, and the fear of being tested. It demands that we trade the safety of the insulated expert for the vulnerability of the genuine listener.

Design Democracy is not just a theoretical framework; it's a hard-won philosophy grounded in personal experience. I didn't learn the most important lessons about design in an architecture studio; I learned them on the lonely highways of a cross-country bicycle journey and in the disciplined, sweat-soaked struggle of a martial arts dojo. From these experiences, I learned that true empathy isn't an intellectual exercise; it's a visceral understanding born from shared struggle.

Pedaling against a demoralizing headwind for hours on end, stripped of all privilege and reliant on my own resilience and the kindness of strangers, I learned that progress is measured in Slow Wins. In the ring, I learned that the only way to control fear is to face it directly, to get "punched in the face," literally and metaphorically, and realize that the pain is survivable, an invaluable lesson. These experiences taught me that the principles for building a resilient self are the very same ones we need to build our most meaningful spaces.

In this book, I'll show you how to put that philosophy into practice. I'll make the case for a "Predictive Placemaking" approach, proving that an empathy-driven process is not a concession but a formidable business strategy that delivers a measurable return on investment. Just as the Oakland A's used statistics to find undervalued players, Design Democracy uses data to unlock the most undervalued asset in any organization: the collective intelligence and authentic needs of its people. The story of the Newmark Knight Frank headquarters in Los Angeles will be our central case study, showing how this exact process transformed a traditional real estate firm, de-risked their massive investment, and resulted in a space that demonstrably increased both employee attendance and per-person revenue.

But before we leap into the application and nuances of Design Democracy, we'll first deconstruct the failures of the old guard, exposing the myths behind traditional design methods and the systemic issues within the commercial real estate industry. Next, we will go through a practical playbook for implementing Design Democracy, detailing the tools, techniques, and leadership mindset it requires. We will then explore the messy reality of the work itself, offering strategies for troubleshooting hang-ups as well as harnessing the Tough Empathy needed to navigate a project to completion. Finally, we will explore the ultimate choice that lies at the heart of this work, the choice to reject the safety of the critic and embrace the courageous, vulnerable path of the creator. That is the ultimate journey of building better spaces and, in the process, building a better self.

Chapter 1:

Confronting Fear - Finding Dragons

You know those old maps, the ones with elaborate drawings of sea monsters and dragons in the margins? Cartographers would write "Here be dragons" at the edges of the world they hadn't explored. These weren't just doodles or catchy sayings; these markings symbolized a very human feeling: being scared of the unknown. The mapmaker, sitting comfortably in their studio, could only guess what was out there, their minds filling in the blanks with the worst-case scenario. Dragons, giant squids, you name it.

For architects, designers, and their clients, every new project is a blank spot on the map. That empty screen, that tricky problem we haven't solved yet, that's where our dragons live. We fill in the unknowns with little voices of self-doubt, the fear of failing, the anxiety of being judged, and that one big question that gets all of us: *What if I'm just not good enough?*

This chapter is your invitation to sail into these uncharted waters, to explore the shared borders of fear and design. We'll learn how to spot the dragons hiding on the periphery of experience, understand what they're trying to say, and see them as signs that you're actually heading in the right direction. When you feel that fear of the unknown, it means you're at the edge of your comfort zone, and that's where all the good stuff happens. We'll face fear not as an enemy, but as a compass that points us toward real growth and empathy. Charting new territory, fear and all, is what it means to be a designer, developer, and client alike.

Design Fear: The Unwanted Feature

To get a handle on fear, we first have to get why it exists. Fear isn't a glitch in our system; it's a feature that's been hardwired into us for ages to keep us alive. When our ancestors ran into a saber-toothed tiger, they didn't have time to think things through. Their brain's alarm system would just take over. A rush of adrenaline would get the body ready to either fight for its life or run away. Fear is the reason we're all here today.

The only problem is that our alarm system hasn't evolved as fast as our intellect. It can't readily or reliably tell the difference between facing a tiger and encountering a complicated design challenge. The stakes are different, of course, but the fear can feel nearly identical. That's just the brain doing its job, trying to protect you from what it *thinks* is a threat.

So, what's the threat within design? Obviously, we're not about to get eaten, but our egos might sense imminent death, our sense of being good at what we do might feel threatened, and we might be worried about how others see us. All of these are very real threats. In fact, design and development have a few pervasive fear problems:

The threat of the unknown
> Design is all about making sense of a mess. You have to step into a place where there are few patterns in order to spot new ones. Breaking away from the known is difficult for our individual brains and difficult for groups of stakeholders too.

The threat of judgment
> When you design or commission something, you're putting a piece of your thinking out there for the whole world to see. A building, an office interior, a new hospital, they're not just drawings; they're a part of you. So, when your research points you in a controversial direction, it feels especially risky to follow these clues. *Will they think I'm not good enough?* is a pervasive, circling question that hovers over every decision.

The threat of confrontation
> Since the design process involves so many individuals and objectives, it's easy to feel cornered and resort to aggressive responses when our work is questioned or criticized. To regain our perceived lack of control, we might lash out, make accusations, or initiate a conflict, all to avoid the threat of confrontation.

Every time you create something, you're making yourself vulnerable. Every new project is a real risk. You're on the frontlines of seeing the future for someone else, your client or your employees. You're answering questions before there's enough information to answer them fully. Your brain tells you to do the safe thing . . . "Let's make this law firm just like the last one," or "I want my tech firm to look just like Google's because that's what's in the news." But these usually aren't the right choices. The right choice is often the scary one. This is why getting a handle on fear isn't just a nice-to-have skill for design projects; it's a must-have.

If you're not willing to face the fear of innovation, you're not ready to design. This is because real innovation demands that we dismantle the comfort of design privilege and engage in the messy, human work of asking difficult questions. A simple query like, "How often do you come to the office, and what do you do when you are there?" can feel confrontational to both parties. The person answering fears the consequences of an honest answer, a perfect example of preference falsification. But the leader asking must also confront fear, the fear of hearing an inconvenient truth that might challenge their entire vision. The willingness to push through this mutual discomfort is what separates a mediocre project from a transformative one; it's the gateway to the authentic data that allows true innovation to emerge.

The Cost of Inaction

Imagine an architect and their client who let fear run the show. What do their projects look like? They look like every other project, template after template, times a million. They use the same old formulas, the same old templates, and the same old solutions. They never question assumptions or push back on fashionable standards. They don't learn new collaboration software because that initial struggle is just too uncomfortable. They don't like working with others because it means showing their messy, half-finished ideas. The work they do is . . . fine. But it rarely solves underlying problems, rarely reflects a company's unique culture, and rarely inspires. These designers aren't really designing anymore; they're just copying themselves.

What's the biggest price we pay for listening to fear? Mediocrity. Mediocrity builds us a nice, cozy little cage made of repeated versions of ourselves. The real value we could provide is within reach but never seized. It lies within the magic of asking questions, exploring alternate directions, and connecting ideas in new ways. Fear shuts all of that down. It narrows our focus to just one thing: not failing.

When we're working from a place of fear:

We stop learning.

To really learn, we have to admit when we don't know something. We have to fight against the temptation to push our views forward or tout our knowledge based solely on our past clients and past experiences. Instead of defending our expertise at every turn, we can put that extra energy into listening and asking questions.

We avoid risk.

We can't innovate without taking risks. The best design solutions often come from looking at problems from a variety of angles. *Listen, observe, measure.* Take this comprehensive approach to problem-solving, not just with one person, but with the entire design team. Collecting information from everyone involved in the project is daunting and seems risky, but it's the secret to finding design essence, the opposite of mediocrity.

We lose our voice.

Good design has a point of view. It uses evidence to stand up for the user, to explain design choices, and to navigate a client to the right place. Fear just wants us to be agreeable and quiet. But if we follow fear's lead, we end up simply parroting back what we think people want to hear.

We isolate ourselves.

Fear loves it when we're alone. It tells us that the fewer people who are involved in the design, the less criticism it (and, by proxy, we) will receive. That isolated design will also contain less truth and therefore offer less value, but fear keeps these outcomes on the down-low.

Getting over fear doesn't mean charging recklessly ahead. It means getting more comfortable with being uncomfortable. It means experiencing the inherent anxiety and uncertainty within design as signals of growth, not stop signs. The goal is to feel the fear and do that scary thing anyway. Because everything you want, every new skill, every cool solution, every bit of professional growth, is waiting for you on the other side of that feeling. Staying in the safe harbor means you'll rarely encounter dragons, sure, but it also means you'll never discover new worlds.

How do we practice sailing into uncharted territory? We can certainly do it at the drafting table, but sometimes that's not close enough to the seat of fear. That's not really where the fear originates, so it can be hard to solve there. We need some real exposure therapy to find the locus of our fear and condition ourselves to deal with it directly. Sometimes that exposure comes from unexpected places, far from the drafting table. For me, it happened in the ring.

Seconds before getting in the ring, I learned I would be fighting someone thirty years younger than me. This kid, soon to be a college football player, had trained in Denver, Colorado. *He probably has a third lung*, my fear was shouting at me.

Three rounds of Muay Thai for three minutes each doesn't sound like a long time, but believe me, it's an eternity when you're standing inside those ropes. I made my weight earlier that morning at 169 pounds, and I was feeling ready. I was hydrated, and I'd had enough to eat. Now it was showtime, and I felt a little different. *What did I get myself into?* I kept thinking, mildly terrified at the news that I'd be facing someone three decades younger.

At that point, about to literally "take it on the chin," I recalled the personal and professional development books I'd read, *Do Hard Things* by Steve Magness, *The Comfort Crisis* by Michael Easter, *Can't Hurt Me* by David Goggins, all telling me to try harder and get harder. Maybe this time I'd taken it too far. No amount of reading had prepared me for getting kicked in the ribs. But there was no backing out now.

In theory, I knew how to avoid every punch and combo. I was prepped for every situation. I stayed light on my feet, and then *POW*. . . stars. I start to think maybe I've been reading a bit too much David Goggins. He says I have another untapped forty percent, and I think he's right. After all, I've been training relentlessly for this fight for ten years, and I'm still getting stronger. Stronger on the inside and out.

I promise I'll get back to this fight, but what does it have to do with design? Well, this was my extreme way of confronting fear again and again, and of finding a path toward a deeper level of empathy. I figured that by engaging in activities that defied privilege, where there was no advantage given for wealth or class, I would develop authenticity, and with that authenticity, a reduction in everyday fear.

And I was right. These self-imposed challenges, tests, and adventures gave me the truth I needed. This new sense of reality had other gifts as well. An increased ability to not only manage fear, but a broader ability to empathize, too. These gifts would help me shape the foundations of what would become Design Democracy.

This was the real breakthrough. I became far less afraid of design failure because I faced an even bigger fear, of getting kicked in the face. You don't need to take this lesson as far as I did to get the value of confronting fear. I'd argue that taking up surfing or Tai Chi would work just as well as stepping into a ring. Overcoming the fear of breaking into a new activity, of getting uncomfortable and learning a skill, all of this leads to greater comfort and freedom from the mediocrity at our core. The mediocrity that warns us of dragons when, instead, we can set off into the unknown and learn to harness their fire-breathing powers.

Chapter 2:

Enterprise-Level Empathy - The Architect and the Ghost

Imagine an architect hired to design a growing company's new headquarters. He's brilliant. His portfolio contains stunning, award-winning structures. He studies the building site and the angle of the sun, and he includes the finest sustainable materials. He draws up breathtaking renderings with clean lines, soaring ceilings, and elegant spaces. On paper, it's a perfect office space.

But our architect has a secret. He's afraid of messy conversations. He finds the chaotic, unpredictable nature of company culture, the differing opinions, the interdepartmental workstyles, and the hierarchical seating arrangements to be deeply uncomfortable. He avoids contractors. He never meets the employees who will be using the space. He reads a list of initial needs, notes the desired number of offices, and then retreats to the safety of his studio. He designs for a theoretical "company," an idealized client who exists only in his imagination, and he assumes the use of the space will conform to his vision.

When the company moves in, the problems begin. The beautiful, office-lined perimeter, perfect for law firms of the past, becomes a barrier to natural light and innovation. The singular coffee break kitchen defies the collaborative hospitality needs of multiple divisions within a growing, creative firm. The one-size-fits-all conference room restrains the tech-driven style of small group work. The office is a masterpiece of aesthetics, but it is a failure as architecture for a specific company culture. It is a monument to the architect's taste, but also to his fear. He designed a solution for a problem he never took the time to truly understand. He designed for a ghost.

This is the central challenge at the heart of all design. Whether you are creating a website, a chair, a software application, a service, or a skyscraper, you are not merely arranging pixels, bending wood, or writing code. You are solving both a production problem and a human problem. And you cannot solve a problem you do not understand on a deeply visceral, empathetic level.

Design, in its purest form, is a visual and tangible act of empathy. It is the process of seeing the world through another's eyes and designing just the right thing to accommodate that vision with your strengths. Empathy-powered design streamlines the removal of barriers and creates onramps to innovation. Each user-driven design solution is a bridge to a better user experience.

But empathy is not a soft skill we are simply born with or without. It is a muscle. And for many of us, it has atrophied, unused due to our own fears, comforts, and privileges. To be a truly great designer, we must first become a courageous one. We must be willing to step out of the clean, well-lit studio of our own experience and into the messy, complicated, and often uncomfortable world of the teams we're working with and people we're designing for.

In this chapter, we'll explore how to develop the courage to see so you can design solutions that are both beautiful and profoundly human.

Design is Empathetic Problem-Solving

Let's dismantle the common myth that design is primarily about aesthetics. This is like saying cooking is primarily about arranging food on a plate. Presentation matters, of course, but it is the outcome of a much deeper process. The real work of a chef is in understanding ingredients, balancing flavors, and delegating tasks in the kitchen to create a nourishing and delightful experience. The plating is the final flourish.

So too with design. The visual form a solution takes—the colors, the materials, the layout—is the final expression of a long chain of pattern finding and problem-solving. The real work of a designer is to uncover the following unknowns:

- What is the user trying to accomplish?
- What is frustrating them? What is blocking their path?
- What does their world feel, sound, and look like?
- What is the unspoken need, the latent desire they can't articulate?

Just as important, the designer can only succeed if the project is grounded in the following realities:

- What is the budget and project timeline?
- What are the critical schedule needs and milestones?
- How will they build within these constraints?

Answering these questions is not an intellectual exercise. Data can tell you *what* is happening, but it rarely tells you *why*. The "why" lives in the realm of human experience, and the only key to unlock it is empathy.

Empathy in design means feeling the user's frustration when technology is confusing. It means experiencing the anxiety of someone trying to navigate a complex healthcare system through a reception area you've built. It means sharing that small spark of delight a user feels when a conference room reservation tool works exactly as they hoped, almost as if it read their mind.

When you operate from this empathetic core, your role shifts. You are no longer a decorator applying a veneer of "good design" to a pre-existing product. You're a detective, a psychologist, and an advocate all in one. You are fighting for your partners, your team, and the user at every turn. Your design decisions become a form of visual problem-solving, where every choice is a direct response to an empathetic insight.

With empathy, your design work transforms:

Your language on the very first page of your drawings is clear.
Yes, it satisfies the permitting requirements, but you also understand that the builder needs clear instructions to get started.

Your list of materials is refined.
You're not a minimalist; you just want to minimize mistakes and make the purchasing process easy for the furniture vendor and the client to approve.

Your shared folder of plans is chronological.
You want to make it easy for vendors and clients alike to both see the history of design and coordinate new engineering with the latest information.

Empathy is the understanding. Design is the physical solution. Without empathy, design is just decoration for a ghost client and their imagined needs.

The Fear That Blinds Us

If empathy is the engine of great design, fear is the hand that reaches for the emergency brake. It is the most powerful barrier between us and the people we serve because it tells us to stay safe, to stick with what we know, and to avoid the discomfort of the unknown at all costs.

As a designer, you face a unique constellation of fears. There's the fear of failure, that your brilliant idea will fall flat, that users will hate it, that you'll be exposed as an imposter. There's the fear of criticism, the sting of negative feedback from a client, a boss, or a user test. There's the fear of not being creative enough, of staring at a blank page and feeling a complete void of ideas.

But the most profound fear, the one that cuts off empathy at its root, is the fear of the unknown. It is the fear of stepping into a world you do not understand.

This is where privilege becomes a powerful obstacle. In the context of design, privilege is the bubble of our own default experience. For many of us, that includes the privilege of being able to see without assistance, to hear clearly, to walk without pain, to navigate the digital world with ease, to understand the cultural context a product is built for. It is the privilege of not having the problem we are trying to solve.

Privilege provides us with the excuse to stay outside the problem—to not immerse ourselves in a world where that privilege no longer exists—and fear motivates us to stay put. This combination is lethal to empathy. It keeps us designing for ourselves, or for the ghost-client who is just like us. It ensures that our solutions, while perhaps technically proficient, will lack the soul and insight that come only from genuine connection. We can't see the problem clearly because we're too afraid to look.

For too long, the people in charge of commissioning new spaces, executives, managers, and even seasoned architects, have operated from within this bubble of design privilege. This is the unexamined belief that their experience, taste, and authority give them a unique insight into what an organization needs. They gather in a boardroom, look at a few glossy images, and make multi-million-dollar decisions with little to no authentic input from the people who will actually live and work in the space. The result is an environment that reflects the preferences of a powerful few, not the collective needs of the many.

So, how do we break out of this design privilege? How do we pop the bubble?

The answer comes from a counterintuitive place: clinical psychology, and the practice of exposure therapy. The principle behind exposure therapy is simple: to overcome a fear, we must confront it in a controlled, gradual, and repeated way.

The main barrier in my design journey was the fear of being challenged. It was about 2004, I was about five years into my career, accomplished at this point, but still new to design leadership. I was already being tasked with developing design strategies for complex organizations, and I had a good sense of what was needed to make better spaces. Or at least I thought I did, from the safety of my office. There, I could converse with leaders, look at data, consume research, and form ideas. But I was not very connected to the actual users of the space. I talked with CEOs and their senior leaders, but I already suspected that spaces driven solely by these people were often beautiful failures. Already, I was asking questions: What did the lawyer really need from their office? How did the doctor use their exam rooms? What was the workflow of the computer programmer? But since I was rarely given access to these people, I didn't know the answers.

How could I expose myself to these industries in an accurate and efficient way? The goal, after all, wasn't to become a lawyer, a doctor, or a programmer. My goal was to understand their processes, patterns, and *struggles*. To really empathize with their experiences and to design for *them*.

I knew I needed my own form of exposure therapy to reach this goal. I knew that my privileges had prevented me from learning through adversity; New England boarding school and the Ivy League made sure of this. I thought back to when I was in design school, when my experiences in a New England boarding school and the Ivy League left me feeling disconnected from most people's everyday reality. So, I decided to couple design school with the jobsite. This was the only way to introduce reality and grit to an otherwise silver-spoon path. Each summer in the 90s, I'd spent eight weeks framing houses to the tunes of Casey Kasem's Top 40. The experience was humbling, frustrating, and deeply illuminating. No one cared what school I went to, or the brilliance of my drawings; what mattered was how accurately I could cut a straight line and how fast I could carry a pile of plywood from the first to the second floor.

The day-to-day realities of the jobsite, the smoke break chit chat, the beers on a Friday afternoon, these things shaped me in ways design school never could. I started absorbing critical insights that I would only appreciate fully years later. I learned how the assembly of the building worked. I learned how joists, studs, and rafters were nailed together. I learned how to wire J boxes and find pathways for ventilation ducting. I learned the sequence of the jobsite. I learned the flow of the guys in the field. I learned that when drawings suck, people don't use them, and when the plans are lean and clear, they accelerate and improve the process of building.

By working hands-on with materials and tools I designed for, and discovering just how difficult it was, I developed a new, authentic empathy for the professionals who do it flawlessly every day. Genuine respect and a list of a dozen real-world problems that needed solving replaced my fear of not knowing how drawings transformed into 3D spaces. I could now have a conversation with every trade worker, not as an expert, but as a humble student. I could ask intelligent questions. The barrier of my fear and privilege had been broken, not by pretending to be an expert but by becoming an expert beginner.

You are not aiming for mastery in breaking out of design privilege. You are aiming for understanding. The goal is to replace your assumptions with empathy. That's it. Each of these acts is a form of exposure therapy, chipping away at the fear of the unknown and deflating the bubble of privilege. The process is often inefficient, awkward, and humbling. And it is the single most valuable design research you will ever do.

This empathy for the field made me a better architect in so many ways, and it eventually helped me empathize with the user of space as well. I didn't have to be the lawyer or doctor using the space to understand their challenges and needs because I had learned how to humble myself to try to see the world the way they did, and ask about their specific challenges. I could blend the realities I knew about construction with empathy for the user to develop the truth in architecture.

Design for People, Not Ghosts

Let's return to our architect. Imagine if he had started the design process differently. Imagine if he hadn't begun with drawings but instead, started by listening to the users and conducting anonymous surveys aimed at unearthing honest user experiences. Imagine if the designer had studied their poorly lit internal conference rooms, witnessed the workers struggling with their collaboration technology, and counted badging data to see that only twenty-five percent of the staff regularly reported for duty. *A complete guide to this data-gathering methodology can be found in the Design Democracy Playbook in Appendix B.*

If he had approached the project this way before drawing anything, our architect would've uncovered the company's frustration with their conference space, their struggle with the current technology, and their desire for a spacious, well-lit office. He would have quickly learned their unspoken needs, and his fear of the messiness of their lives would have been replaced by an empathetic connection.

When he returned to the studio, our architect would no longer be designing for a ghost. He would be designing for real people. For a growing company that depends on technology-driven meetings of all sizes. For a sales-driven, growth-oriented company that has very few executives in the office full-time. For lifestyle-focused workers who successfully balance work in the office with work on the road and at home. The office he designs to fulfill the needs of these people might look different than what he'd come up with if he had started with those neat, clean drawings, perhaps a little less minimalist, a little more practical, but it would be a true innovation center. It would be a masterpiece, not just of architecture but of empathy.

This is our calling as designers and company leaders. It is not a common path. It demands that we intentionally and repeatedly step into worlds that are not our own. It requires us to have the humility to listen, to admit what we don't know, and to feel the user's frustration in our own soul.

We must choose to design without fear. We must find the courage to pop the bubble of our own privilege and experience the world as others do. We must do the hard, humbling, and transformative work of building empathy so that we can design for real people, in all their beautiful, messy, and complex glory.

The world has enough beautiful objects designed for ghosts. What it needs are more thoughtful, compassionate, and courageous solutions designed for us.

Case Study:

A Cautionary Tale of Design Privilege—When design privilege or expertise privilege of any kind goes unchecked, the result is a massive investment in a beautiful but empty vessel. I saw this with a prominent apparel brand. With three famous architecture firms and a CEO with a singular vision, they built a stunning 300-person office. The only problem? They never consulted a single employee. Eight years later, the average daily attendance is just 31 people. This is the predictable outcome when a design process is a monologue instead of a dialogue. (See Case Study 1 in Appendix A.)

Chapter 3:

The Stardust of Innovation

It was 2013, I'd been married three years, and I had a one-year-old girl and another on the way. I'd been out of design school for fifteen years, succeeding in my career and incrementally leveling up. I was a bit less combative and a bit more collaborative. The next step might require moving to another firm. I needed a place that would commit to the ideas of Design Democracy. I landed a position at Newmark Knight Frank, a company with a huge global presence in real estate and all the associated consulting prowess I was looking for. I was certain I was making this upward career move into a company that shared my vision for collaborative design and the idealized relationship I imagined between the real estate transactions they made and the real estate projects I would take on. I started in July of that year.

Later that year, when they asked me to lead the design and construction of their new downtown Los Angeles headquarters, I gladly accepted. The project offered me the perfect laboratory to test my core belief: that data, measurement, and consensus—the foundations of what eventually became Design Democracy—were the future of project consulting. This was my chance to establish credibility and prove that our physical environments shouldn't be a byproduct of habit but rather a strategic tool forged from the reality of our collective needs.

From the very beginning, I was handed a set of contradictory directions. In one breath, I was told to give special consideration to the brokerage teams, the firm's highest-earning and most vocal group, and make the new office's overall layout roughly the same as the old one. In the next breath, I was expected to innovate and find new ways to increase profits for the firm. These two directives would be difficult to reconcile.

To me, tradition is different from culture. I never want to ignore tradition, as it has its place, but it's only fractionally as important as culture. Culture is the reality of *now*. Tradition is the reality of the past. I was, and still am, dedicated to the study of culture, the study of the present. But there I was, at the start of a landmark project, dealing with people and directions that were in sharp conflict with every part of my system. Unlike today, when I can simply choose to not work with clients who don't share this ethos, this was my direct employer, and I would be designing the office where I would sit for years.

The questions loomed large: What should I do? Go along with the status quo, build a pretty but ultimately dysfunctional monument to the past? Or use this project as an opportunity to show Design Democracy to the people who could help it scale, who could help me spread its true power?

I chose the latter. This chapter is about what I learned through that process, and what it reveals about the profound, often underestimated power of design. It's about how the spaces we inhabit are not passive containers but active participants in our work, our lives, and our potential.

The project was ultimately a success, but not without its share of drama.

What Great Design Actually Accomplishes

We've all felt it. The quiet focus of a grand library, the energetic buzz of a bustling coffee shop, the calming serenity of a minimalist spa. Beautifully designed environments have the power to elevate our mood and productivity. This isn't just a vague, esoteric feeling; it's a tangible, measurable phenomenon. Great design works on us psychologically and physiologically, shaping our thoughts, behaviors, and even our well-being. It's the invisible architecture that supports our best selves.

When we think of "beautiful design," we often default to aesthetics—the pleasing color palette, the elegant furniture, the dramatic lighting. But true beauty in design is the seamless marriage of form and function. A space is only truly beautiful if it *works*. It's beautiful because it anticipates your needs, because it makes a complex task feel effortless, because it quiets the noise of the world and allows you to think. It fosters connection when you need it and provides sanctuary when you don't.

But in the Newmark project, the initial push I received from leadership was for a design that privileged a select few. The "beautiful" office they envisioned had a wing of large, impressive private offices for the brokers, a physical manifestation of hierarchy and tradition, and a vision of beauty based on ego. But our company data told a different story, one that would drastically change this imagined design. The highest-ranking people, the brokers, spent the least amount of time in the office. They were road warriors; their success happened in the field, not in a private office. A design that gave them sprawling, empty offices would not only be a colossal waste of space and money; it would also fail to be truly beautiful. Why? Because it would be dysfunctional. It would ignore the reality of their work, and everyone else's.

Conversely, some of the most critical administrative teams, like marketing and financial services, were constantly in the office. Their work was collaborative and detailed, and they required specific adjacencies and resources. The office was mission control for them. Great design, in this context, meant creating a space that empowered *them*. It meant giving them the light, the technology, and the collaborative zones they needed to excel. The old model, the "bad design," had relegated these vital teams to the functional-but-uninspired corners of the office, which in turn hampered their potential and, by extension, the entire firm's productivity.

Great design accomplishes this shift from ego to empathy. It uses data to understand the true story of an organization and crafts a physical narrative to match. The result is an environment that doesn't just look good but *feels* right, because it is aligned with a company's authentic culture and workflow. This kind of design elevates mood by reducing friction and frustration. It boosts productivity by providing the right tools in the right places for the right people. It replaces a monument to the past with a platform for the future.

And that's exactly what I wanted to do with Newmark's new Los Angeles headquarters. I just needed to convince them that my process would work.

Commercial Spaces as Strategic Business Levers

For too long, corporate real estate has been viewed through a narrow lens: a line item on a balance sheet, a cost to be minimized. The space a company occupies is considered a necessary evil, not a strategic asset. But this is a profound and costly misunderstanding. A thoughtfully designed commercial space is one of the most powerful, albeit underutilized, tools a company has to reach its most critical business objectives.

Think about the primary goals of any ambitious company: attract and retain top talent, foster innovation, increase productivity, build a strong brand identity, and drive profitability. A bland, uninspired office actively works against these objectives, whereas a dynamic, purpose-built environment actively accelerates them.

The Newmark project became a perfect case study in this principle. The initial directive to maintain the same square footage was based on a flawed, cost-centric view of the office. But my Design Democracy data—the surveys, movement studies, and deep listening interviews—proved a startling hypothesis: we needed *less* space per person, but a completely *different kind* of space, with vastly different attributes.

When my team listened to everyone equally, we were able to design an office that functioned like a finely tuned machine for performance, not a warehouse for people. The brokers got smaller, private "touchdown" spaces for when they did come into the office. The collaborative teams received dynamic project rooms and open, flexible work zones. We supported quiet, heads-down work with dedicated focus pods and library-like areas. In short, we tailored the environment to the *work*, not the job title.

The business results were staggering. First, the most obvious: huge savings on rent. By shedding unnecessary square footage, we reduced one of the company's largest fixed costs by thirty-two percent, freeing up capital that could be reinvested in talent, technology, or client services. Second, we saw the *right kind* of office utilization increase. The people who truly needed office resources, the administrative and support teams, came in more and were more effective while there. Their satisfaction and productivity soared. Third, the brokers, liberated from the expectation of occupying a large, symbolic office, spent more time generating business in the field.

The new Los Angeles headquarters became a physical manifestation of the company's brand and vision. It silently and consistently communicated a message of intelligence, efficiency, and focus. It told potential new hires that this company invested in its people's actual needs, not in outdated symbols of status.

In this way, the office transformed from a passive cost center into an active catalyst for business success. It wasn't just a place where work happened; it was a tool that made the work, and the entire business, better.

There was also a sharp change in how those same brokers perceived my value. It was no longer an abstract concept. They felt the benefit of Design Democracy in their daily work. This was the tangible result of overcoming preference falsification; sure, their individual offices were smaller, but the design gave them more of everything they authentically needed. The process had broken down the very silos that created friction, putting the people and resources they relied on in perfect proximity for the kind of collaboration that closes deals.

This success fundamentally shifted my role. I was no longer fighting to be included; I was being brought in to lead. The brokers now understood that Design Democracy wasn't just a design process; it was a powerful business development tool. My methodology was featured as the lead concept in new business presentations, transforming it from a "box to check" into our core competitive advantage. This was the ultimate proof of our "Predictive Placemaking" strategy. The teams that embraced the process won business at a higher rate, their deals closed faster, and, adjusted for other factors, Design Democracy accounted for a fifteen percent increase in regional profits in its first year: a total of about $20 million.

A Catalyst for Human Potential

The right space is more than a container for human activity; it's a catalyst for human potential. Just as fertile soil allows a seed to grow, the right environment allows individuals and teams to flourish. It can break down invisible barriers, foster serendipitous encounters, and provide the psychological safety needed for people to do their best, most innovative work. Conversely, the wrong space can stifle creativity, inhibit collaboration, and drain the very energy it's meant to support.

At its core, the philosophy of Design Democracy is about unlocking this potential. It's a rejection of the top-down, "because I said so" approach to design that has dominated the field for centuries. That old model is based on the assumption that a handful of leaders know what's best for everyone. But they rarely do because their perspective is limited. They don't experience the daily friction of a poorly placed printer, the frustration of not having a quiet place for a confidential call, or the missed opportunity for collaboration because teams are siloed on different floors.

The story of the Newmark office is a story of unleashing latent potential. We discovered that the office was far more important for the people whose perspectives were most overlooked: the marketing team, the financial analysts, the administrative staff, the people whose daily effectiveness was most profoundly impacted by the design of their environment. By giving them a platform to be heard, privately and equally through our surveys and data collection, we didn't just gather their preferences. We tapped into a reservoir of institutional knowledge about how work *actually* got done. They knew what they needed, but no one had ever bothered to ask them in a systematic, meaningful way.

When we analyzed the data, it became clear that the kind of space the firm had used in the past wasn't just outdated; it was actively hindering the potential of a huge portion of its workforce. Had I designed based off the original instructions, the new headquarters would have physically represented and reinforced the idea that only the loudest voices, the brokers, mattered to the company. If we had caved to those initial demands, we would have built an office that wouldn't have even worked for them, let alone anyone else.

The new design catalyzed potential in several ways. It created "collision zones"—high-traffic areas like coffee bars, central staircases, and varied lounge spaces, where people from different departments would naturally interact. You can't schedule innovation, but you can design a space that radically increases the odds of a serendipitous conversation that sparks new ideas.

The design also introduced an element of personal choice into a previously straightforward environment. We offered employees a variety of work settings, from bustling collaborative hubs to monastic quiet zones, letting them choose the environment that best suited their task at any given moment. This autonomy turned out to be a powerful driver of engagement and performance. The new space gave employees options, signaling that the company trusted each person to know how they worked best.

Ultimately, the CEO, Barry Gosin, saw this potential in our drawings and understood the justifications generated by the early version of Design Democracy. When the time came to approve the multimillion-dollar design in the face of internal opposition, his words starkly endorsed this new philosophy: "Don't worry about those assholes, they'll either adapt or die." A blunt but accurate assessment. It was incredibly validating to hear this support and to know there was a breed of leadership out there that was quickly attuned to the philosophy of Design Democracy. He immediately understood that clinging to a design that served privilege over performance was, in the long run, a losing strategy for everyone.

The right space, tailored to the needs of the whole and not the wants of the few, became a catalyst that unlocked the collective potential of everyone.

The Universal Language of Bad Design

We all know bad design when we see it and experience it. You don't need a degree in architecture to feel your soul drain out under the flickering fluorescent lights of a windowless office. You don't need to be a user experience expert to feel the spike of frustration when you push on a door that gets pulled open—or is it the opposite? You can never remember which. Bad design is a universal language of friction, confusion, and subtle-to-severe annoyance.

It's the conference room you can never book, and when you finally do, you can't get the projector to work. It's the open-plan office with no quiet spaces, forcing you to wear headphones all day just to concentrate on a simple email. It's the kitchen that's too small, creating a daily, awkward ballet of people maneuvering to the microwave. It's the long, sterile hallways that make you feel like a cog in a machine. It's the beautiful glass-walled meeting room that offers zero acoustic privacy, making every sensitive conversation a public performance.

These designs aren't just minor inconveniences. They are "micro-aggressions" from the building itself. They add up, creating a low-grade, persistent hum of stress and inefficiency that drains our cognitive resources and emotional reserves. Bad design makes simple tasks hard and hard tasks nearly impossible. And it communicates a message of neglect: the organization either doesn't know how its people work, or it simply doesn't care.

With the Newmark project, the path of least resistance led directly toward bad design, design based solely on tradition and templates. Following that path would have meant replicating and even amplifying the flaws of the old space. The new office would have felt "off," but off in that familiar way, where employees simply continued enduring the low-level friction of the space day in and day out—that fundamental disconnect of design from the reality of the work itself.

This is where our data became the antidote to bad design. My intuition told me something was wrong, but data proved it and pointed us toward a solution. The results from our surveys, visualizations, and access studies showed us that we needed something new. They took the vague, collective feeling of "this isn't working" and translated it into undeniable evidence. Only from gathering data did we discover that the brokers were barely in the office, and this was the key that unlocked us from the "bad design" of giving them huge, empty offices. This gave us the political cover to challenge the status quo. Anyone can argue with an opinion; it's much harder to argue with a stack of data that shows just how misaligned opinion can be with reality. I had condensed our attendance data, visual and narrative survey preferences, and usage observations into a 10-page report. This document also contained drawings, budgets, and schedules, the normal planning basics, but it was the data, preferences, and observations that were potent for sharing with local executives, New York leadership, and any other conflicted stakeholders to show that we weren't just flying blind, fueled by trends, but driven by user truth. This report mapped the direct links between user needs and the proposed project design details and made every conversation and presentation more effective at developing consensus.

Bad design is often the product of laziness, fear, and a failure of imagination. It's easier to copy what was done before or lean on trends than to do the hard work of discovering what's needed now. But recognizing bad design is the first step toward creating something great. It's within that friction and frustration that the seeds of a better solution lie waiting.

The Hidden Opportunity in Every Design Project

Every design project, whether it's building a new skyscraper from the ground up or simply reconfiguring a single office, contains a hidden opportunity: uncovering the intangible, asking the deeper questions, using the *process* to change each business and project for the better.

The temptation in any project is to focus on the tangible: walls, furniture, finishes. But the real work, the work that yields exponential returns, is in uncovering these intangibles. It's about asking those deeper questions and zeroing in on the process itself. The project isn't just to build a new office; it's an opportunity to break down departmental silos. The project isn't just to update the aesthetic; it's an opportunity to create a physical manifestation of the brand that inspires employees and wows clients. The project isn't just about accommodating more people; it's an opportunity to design a workflow that makes everyone more efficient and innovative.

Designing a new Newmark headquarters: this was the stated project. The hidden opportunity within it was to use data to dethrone privilege and tradition and prove the value of a new operating system for the design process itself. It was a chance to hold up a mirror to the organization and ask, "Is this who we really are? Is this how we really work?" The data became our flashlight, illuminating the dark corners where inefficiency and inequality were hiding.

The most nuanced and unexpected results are what I call the *stardust of innovation*: the things that are not obvious at the start but emerge like gems in the data. They only reveal themselves under the special conditions of a truly democratic design process, a process of deep listening and receptivity. For us, the stardust was the realization that we could have a more effective, more equitable, and more desirable office in a smaller footprint. This idea was completely counterintuitive to the prevailing real estate logic at the time. It was that single first small pulse of starlight that, once revealed, changed the entire financial and strategic equation of the project.

Nowadays, our process allows the constellation of a culture to reveal itself with remarkable speed, but in those early days, each insight felt like discovering a new planet. Fifteen years ago, the simple idea of making offices smaller and moving them off the perimeter glass was a radical departure from the norm, a direct challenge to the design privilege that treated corner offices as an unquestionable right. Before celebrating this hypothesis or even whispering about the nascent stardust I had found, I knew I had to test it. This idea had to be grounded in data and observation, much like the scientific method, if it was going to succeed. It was these careful, evidence-based steps—which would go on to populate the 10-page report described earlier—that propelled this counterintuitive idea to broad approval and, eventually, expansion across the firm. This hidden opportunity exists everywhere. For a retail store, you're not just contemplating the perfect shelf layout; you're designing a customer journey that keeps customers coming back. For a hospital, you're not just designing patient rooms; you're coming up with a floor plan that reduces nurse fatigue and improves patient outcomes. For a school, you're not just designing classrooms; you're creating spaces that support different learning styles and foster a love of discovery.

To find this hidden opportunity, you must approach every project with a beginner's mind. You must resist the urge to jump to solutions and instead linger in the questions. Treat the project as an archeological dig. The initial brief is just the surface layer. The real treasure, the stardust of innovation, lies buried beneath assumptions and habits. The tools for this excavation are the surveys, conversations, observation, and data analysis you bring to the project. And the act of digging itself, the process of engaging with the people who will use the space, transforms a simple construction project into a catalyst for organizational evolution.

Getting Clear on Your Vision and Transformation

How can Design Democracy transform your projects? The answer to this lies within another, more fundamental question: What are your goals? Before you pick a single paint color, before you look at a single floor plan, you must get radically clear on your vision. A design project without a clear vision is like a ship without a rudder; it will be tossed about by the currents of opinion, budget cuts, and compromise, and will likely end up somewhere no one intended to go.

At Newmark, had I not challenged the norm, the firm would have taken too much space, it would have designed and built the wrong *kind* of spaces, and the lack of justifiable vision would have reflected poorly on a firm that is at least partially charged with seeing the future of real estate.

Transformation doesn't happen by accident. It is the result of intention. Your physical space is one of the most powerful tools you have to manifest that intention. Therefore, the first step in any design process is not about design at all; it's about strategy. It's about defining what success looks like in concrete, human terms.

Start by asking the big questions:
- Why are we doing this project in the first place? (And "because the lease is up" is not a sufficient answer.)
- If this project is wildly successful, what will be different about the business in one year? In five years?
- What behaviors do we want to encourage as a result of this design? More collaboration? More focused work? More informal social interaction?
- What aspects of company culture do we want to amplify? What parts do we want to leave behind?
- How can this space help us attract the kind of talent we need in the future?

In the Newmark project, my vision was clear from the outset: I wanted to use this project as proof of concept for the power of Design Democracy. This clarity of purpose became my compass on the ocean of contradictory directions and political pressure. When I was told to give special consideration to the brokers, my vision forced me to ask, "Why? Will that help us achieve our larger goal of creating a high-performance workplace for *everyone*?" When I was told to keep the square footage the same, my vision prompted another question: "What if our goal isn't to occupy space but to create value? Could we create more value with less space?"

Being clear on my vision helped me distinguish a "want" from a "need." The brokers *wanted* large private offices as symbols of their status. But the data showed us that they didn't *need* them to be effective in their role; in fact, being tied to those offices made them less effective. The company *needed* a space that fostered the productivity of its in-office teams and saved money on rent. A clear vision, backed by data, allowed me to navigate these conflicts and make choices that served the ultimate goal, not just satisfy the loudest voices.

Getting clear on the goals of a project is not a solo activity, because designing isn't a solo activity. It should be a collaborative effort. Engage your leadership team. Engage your employees. Use surveys and conversations to build a shared vision for the future. The final design should be the physical answer to the strategic questions you ask at the beginning. When it is, the space transforms from a mere collection of materials into a partner that constantly and quietly guides an organization toward the future you dared to envision.

Designing for Emotion

After you analyze all the data, set all the strategic goals, and meet all the functional requirements, there remains one final, crucial question before proceeding: What do you want the space to *feel* like? This question moves beyond the purely rational and into the realm of the emotional, the atmospheric, and the intuitive. And while the answer may seem too subjective to be useful, addressing it is one of the most important components of successful design, because how a space makes us feel directly impacts how we behave and perform within it.

The feeling of a space is its soul. Is it energetic and buzzing or calm and focused? Is it sophisticated and formal or playful and approachable? Is it open and transparent or cozy and secure? There are no right or wrong answers, but only a few answers will align with the vision and purpose of a space. A law firm might want to feel solid, trustworthy, and discreet. A tech startup might want to feel innovative, energetic, and transparent. The feeling of a place is part of its function. A space designed for creative brainstorming that feels sterile and intimidating is a failed design.

Articulating the emotion of a place is often the hardest part of the design process for clients. It's difficult to find words for a feeling. This is why referencing imagery is so powerful. A picture, as they say, is worth a thousand words—or at least a few carefully chosen ones. Creating a mood board or a collection of reference images is a critical tool for translating abstract emotional goals into tangible design language. Don't just look at pictures of other offices for inspiration. Look at hotels, restaurants, museums, homes, even natural landscapes. Don't be afraid to combine these images into one collection, either, as each evokes a different feeling, and seeing them together creates yet another.

A photo of a warm, bustling Italian café might capture the feeling of community you want in your breakroom. An image of a serene Japanese garden might inspire the sense of calm you want for a quiet work zone. A picture of a vibrant, colorful street market could inform the dynamic, energetic atmosphere of a collaborative project area. These images create a shared visual vocabulary between you and your design team, ensuring that when you say you want the space to feel "collaborative and energetic," you're all picturing the same thing.

At Newmark, once the data gave us the blueprint—varied spaces, a smaller footprint—we had to pick an aesthetic that felt right. The consensus was clear: the new headquarters should feel sophisticated and professional, befitting a top-tier global firm, but also intelligent and human-centric. The data was against the cold, impersonal feeling of many corporate offices. Every indicator of the feelings we were going for suggested a high-end business club or a boutique hotel as fitting inspirations, places you *wanted* to be. We used a palette of warm woods, rich textures, and dramatic lighting to create this feeling. The final design communicated competence and success without resorting to the old, stuffy language of oversized desks and dark paneling.

Ultimately, the story of the Newmark office is a testament to a simple truth: when we started listening to everyone equally and with empathy, when the minority was able to move past their privilege and consider what the space actually needed, we created something better for everyone. The new space generated huge savings on rent. The right people came into the office more often. And the people who worked the field spent more time doing just that. It was a workplace tailor-made to people's real needs, not merely their privilege or lack thereof. The space had soul, and it felt as good as it functioned, proving that the most powerful designs are those that appeal to our deepest human needs for beauty, purpose, and connection.

Chapter 4:

The Missing Voice in Design

The process of reimagining a company's workplace begins at the top, and it's a scene that has played out in boardrooms and design studios for decades. We, the designers and architects, are summoned to meet with the visionaries—the chief executive officer, who speaks of brand identity and future growth, and the chief financial officer, who outlines the budgetary realities and expectations for return on investment. We listen, we nod, we absorb the high-level strategy. And then, almost invariably, we get ushered down the chain of command. The grand vision is handed off to a committee of division leaders, facility managers, and department heads. This is where the dream meets the harsh, fluorescent-lit reality of corporate politics.

This is the beginning of what I call the *Middle Management Trap*. Over the ensuing weeks and months, the design process deteriorates from a creative, collaborative endeavor into a series of territorial negotiations. We become witnesses, and reluctant referees, to serious power struggles and desperate grabs for space. Each department, convinced of its own supreme importance, argues that its needs are paramount and that the new design should revolve entirely around its workflows. The marketing team needs a collaborative hub for brainstorming sessions. The engineering department demands quiet, focused zones to eliminate distractions. Finance insists on secure, enclosed offices to protect sensitive information.

What begins as level discussion about operational efficiency quickly devolves into a battle for status and validation. A pervasive sense of unfairness begins to fester. Conversations shift from "What kind of space will help us do our best work?" to "Are they getting more than we are?" Suddenly, everyone is counting ceiling tiles, measuring square footage, and scrutinizing floor plans, not for functional merit but as a scorecard of their value to the organization. The corner office, the window view, the proximity to the executive suite, these become coveted prizes in a zero-sum game. Resentment, jealousy, and turf wars cloud over the original vision of a harmonious, innovative workplace like a dense fog. The final design, born from a thousand bitter compromises, often pleases no one. It's a beige monument to a dysfunctional process, a physical manifestation of the organization's internal conflicts.

This traditional, top-down-then-stuck-in-middle-management approach is flawed because it systematically excludes the single most valuable resource in the entire process: the collective wisdom of the people who actually inhabit the space every day. It ignores the stardust of innovation—the constellation of brilliant, practical, and transformative ideas that exist within the workforce if we simply take time to observe. These voices carry untapped potential, but they're missing from the typical design conversation.

At Newmark, I knew right away that focusing only on the "brightest stars"—the senior management and top brokers—would be a fatal mistake. Their view was important, but it was also a perfect expression of design privilege: a perspective heavily oriented toward status and personal profit rather than broader organizational performance. This viewpoint, while a valid data point, couldn't be allowed to drive the entire vision. True innovation, the "stardust" we were looking for, wouldn't come from the corner offices; it would be found in the "missing voices" of the support teams that held the entire operation together. Status and profit are important, but only when balanced with the complete, authentic needs of the whole organization.

This was not a smooth transition. There were fights. Many of the brokers, acting as defenders of the old guard, would overtly say the design vision should be focused exclusively on their wants. I was shouted at and threatened more than a dozen times, a textbook example of the "extra gravity" of the climb. But this is where Tough Empathy becomes critical: our job wasn't to give the most powerful people what they said they wanted, but to discover what the entire organization truly needed to succeed. What they were only able to understand in the end, when our Predictive Placemaking approach was proven right by the data, is that the collective needs of all departments were the stardust. By designing for the marketing team, the finance team, and the project managers, we created a perfect example of the curb cut effect: the brokers became stronger, faster, and more profitable because the very infrastructure of support they relied on was now hyper-efficient, collaborative, and seamlessly integrated into their daily workflow. By removing the daily operational friction for the support staff, we created a frictionless runway for the brokers. They were no longer just individual stars; they were the tip of a highly effective, well-supported spear, and the results spoke for themselves. The facility manager knows where the real bottlenecks are. The administrative assistant has a genius idea for streamlining mail delivery. The junior developer understands the exact type of environment they need to focus. Their insights are not trivial; they are the very building blocks of a truly effective and human-centered workplace. By failing to engage with this collective intelligence, we are not just designing in the dark; we are actively choosing to ignore the light.

When we know this, our challenge as designers is not to find a better way to mediate middle management's power grabs; it's to bypass that trap altogether. How? By changing the very nature of the design process.

The Language Barrier of Design

If the wisdom of the group is so essential, why is it so consistently overlooked? The answer lies in a second, equally formidable obstacle: design is a foreign language to most people. The ecosystem of architecture, construction, and corporate real estate is shrouded in jargon, technical complexities, and unwritten rules that make it feel inaccessible and intimidating to the uninitiated. An employee might have a brilliant idea for how their team's workplace could be improved, but they lack the vocabulary to articulate it in a way that a designer or an executive can understand. They don't know what a "charrette" is, the difference between a "space plan" and a "test fit," or the implications of building codes and ADA regulations.

When people don't speak the language, they feel left out of the conversation. They see designers presenting complex floor plans on a screen, hear them speaking in acronyms and industry terms, and they immediately disengage. They assume, often correctly, that the important decisions have already been made in rooms they weren't invited into. Their potential contribution is silenced before it can even be spoken. This feeling of exclusion is not just a byproduct of the process; it is deeply embedded in the culture of the design profession.

Let's be honest: design can feel high-brow. It's often treated like fine wine or contemporary art—something to be appreciated by a select few with refined tastes but incomprehensible to the average person. This perception is reinforced by the way designers are educated and the culture of the industry they then join. Design school, for all its ability to teach aesthetics, theory, and technical skill, often fails to teach one of the most crucial skills of all: empathy for non-designers. There is a persistent, often unspoken belief within the design community that we, the trained professionals, simply know better than the laypeople we are designing for. This is the "God complex" in architecture, a legacy of the lone genius archetype, the master builder who imposes his singular vision upon the world.

My favorite anecdote on this kicks off the now-famous book *The Wisdom of Crowds* by James Surowiecki, who tells the story of Sir Francis Galton, who, in 1906, studied a contest at a country fair where nearly 800 people guessed the weight of a slaughtered ox. Despite his initial skepticism about collective intelligence, Galton discovered a remarkable outcome after analyzing the guesses. While individual estimates varied greatly, the average (mean) of all the guesses was 1,197 pounds, just one pound off the ox's actual weight of 1,198 pounds. This collective judgment proved to be more accurate than any single individual's guess, including those of experts like butchers and farmers. The experiment became a classic example of the "wisdom of the crowd," demonstrating that the aggregated, independent judgments of a diverse group can be exceptionally intelligent and often superior to that of a single expert.

Industry pressures the artist to further exacerbate this expert mindset. Architects and designers want to create stunning, award-winning portfolio pieces, and all too often, the glossy magazine spread and the vision of an industry award get prioritized over the quiet, everyday functionality of a space. This isn't to say that beauty and function are mutually exclusive, but when the primary goal of a design is creating a monument to the designer's own talent, the actual needs of the users become a secondary concern. The result is a workforce that feels like they're living in someone's art project rather than operating in a space created for them. They are alienated by a process and a profession that speaks a different language, values different things, and operates from a position of prestigious expertise.

To truly unveil the stardust of innovation, we must first translate the language of design into something everyone can understand and participate in.

The Rise of Design Democracy

Breaking free from the Middle Management Trap and overcoming the language barrier of design requires a radical shift in mindset. We must move away from the traditional model of designing *for* people and embrace a new paradigm of designing with people. This is the core principle of Design Democracy.

At first glance, adopting this paradigm may seem like accepting mayhem into the design process, so it's crucial to clarify what Design Democracy is not. It is not a chaotic free-for-all where every decision, from the color of the carpets to the brand of the coffee maker, is put to popular vote. That would be inefficient and would almost certainly lead to a disjointed, incoherent result. Rather, Design Democracy is a structured, facilitated process for making the language of design accessible to empower entire organizations to participate meaningfully in the creation of their own environment. Design Democracy moves us from design dictatorship into collaborative dialogue.

In this new model, the role of the designer undergoes a fundamental transformation. They are no longer the all-knowing expert who delivers a finished, untouchable solution from on high. They become, instead, a facilitator, a translator, and a guide toward a collaborative solution, built from the ground up. Their primary job is not to be the sole decision-maker; it is to make the decisions *easier* for the group.

They become stewards of the process, responsible for creating safe and inclusive spaces for sharing ideas. They translate the complex technical constraints—the budget, the building codes, the construction schedule—into understandable choices with clear trade-offs. They use tools, workshops, and interactive exercises to elicit the hidden knowledge and latent desires of the workforce.

The interactive way in which we collect data as part of the Design Democracy process builds what we call *Evidence-Based Empathy*. We break down the traditional, formal barriers between "designer" and "user" and create a shared foundation for problem-solving. In these sessions, the quiet accountant who has a brilliant idea for a new filing system feels just as empowered to contribute to the design as the outspoken sales director with far more clout. The conversations shift from "I want a bigger office" to "We need a better way to collaborate on confidential documents." The focus moves from defending personal territory and individual value to shared purpose and collaborative success.

This is the process that truly uncovers the stardust of innovation. Once we give people the tools they need to communicate and the permission they need to dream, their ingenuity is boundless and often a welcome surprise. They will devise solutions to problems we didn't even know existed before talking with them. They will see opportunities for connection and efficiency that would never be visible in our standard architectural drawings. And our designs will be better as a result.

By democratizing the design process, we are not abdicating our expertise as designers; we are augmenting it with the lived experience of hundreds of other experts, the experts of their own jobs. We are moving from a single, limited point of view to a rich, multi-faceted understanding of the organization as a living, breathing organism.

The Fruits of Inclusive Design

When we give people a genuine voice in the creation of their workplace, the results are transformative for the entire organization, and the benefits extend far beyond creating a more pleasant and functional office.

First and foremost, the final design is more efficient and more aligned with the actual workflows of a company because the spaces designed through the Design Democracy process are not based on abstract organizational charts or hierarchical assumptions but on a deep understanding of how work actually gets done at that company. As a result, the flow of movement through the space is intuitive and frictionless, and the space itself is more like a high-performance tool than a holding container.

Second, the process itself builds invaluable social capital. When we invite employees to participate, it sends them a powerful message: your voice matters, your experience is valued, and your contribution is essential to the success of this company. Being heard and respected is a massive driver of morale and engagement throughout the workforce. The Middle Management Trap, characterized by resentment and suspicion, gets replaced by a sense of shared ownership and collective pride. When the project is complete, people are not just moving into a new office; they are moving into *their* office, a place they helped create. When people feel this sense of ownership, they are more likely to care for the space, respect the new protocols, and champion the changes to their colleagues. This buy-in is critical for the long-term success of any new design.

Third, and perhaps most importantly, an inclusive design process can be a catalyst for broader organizational innovation. The conversations that take place during the design discovery often have lasting effects that transcend the physical space. As teams discuss how their environment can better support their work, they inevitably start questioning the work itself. They begin to rethink their processes, their communication patterns, and their methods of collaboration. The design process reflects the organization back to itself and prompts a deeper conversation about its culture and its future, actively shaping a new, more collaborative, and more innovative one.

The success of the Newmark project, achieved by confronting fear in the face of immense career risk, emboldened me to push this idea out into the world. It was the ultimate validation that following trends or leadership whims might get you pretty pictures, but it won't get you a strategic tool for success. Since Newmark, I've brought Design Democracy to hundreds of clients, and our Predictive Placemaking model proves time and again that no two law firms, accounting firms, or doctor's offices are the same. Almost every engagement begins with a brief, uncomfortable period of challenging design privilege, but then the process works its magic: the stardust of individual insights begins to form a brilliant new constellation, design becomes almost effortless, and the entire organization rises to meet its own, authentic vision. Ultimately, a workplace designed through a democratic process becomes a strategic asset, not just an overhead cost on a balance sheet. It is an investment in the productivity, well-being, and engagement of a company's most valuable resource: its people. In a world where the war for top talent is fiercer than ever, a workplace designed with and for its people gives organizations a profound competitive advantage, and the return on that investment can't be measured in square feet or ceiling tiles.

The Middle Management Trap is real, but the escape route is clear. We just have to be willing to open the door and invite everyone into the conversation.

A complete guide to this data-gathering methodology can be found in the Design Democracy Playbook in Appendix B.

Case Study:

The Power of Listening—This is not just a theory; it is a proven strategy for unlocking incredible, tangible value. We saw this with a large nonprofit that fully embraced this philosophy for their new 80,000-square-foot headquarters. Because their own culture was based on listening and empathy, they understood the power of gathering the "stardust" from their entire organization. The results were staggering. By systematically listening, we designed a space that not only increased daily office occupancy by six times, but also allowed them to avoid taking costly additional space that would have killed the entire deal. It is the ultimate proof that the most brilliant design solutions are not invented in a boardroom; they are discovered by listening to the constellation of voices within. (See Case Study 2 in Appendix A.)

Chapter 5:

Transactional Design

As usual, we were late to the game, but not for lack of trying. The broker who navigated this deal with me has since become one of my favorites in the industry, a sharp and intuitive partner I'd trust with any transaction. But on this particular deal, we hadn't yet found our stride. Our interactions were bumpy. Both of us were fairly new to running our own companies, having worked together for years at a large firm before separately striking out on our own. We were still learning how to dance together, and this deal was a complicated tango.

Our client, a sprawling organization we had consulted for over several years, was finally ready to commit to a new headquarters. This decision was the culmination of years of analysis, strategic planning, and internal debate. Yet, at many of the most critical steps, my firm and I were left out of the process. The transaction team—a familiar cast of company leaders, landlords, and brokers—operated on a traditional, tightly controlled timeline. They believed, as many still do, that the delicate process of securing a lease is best done in a sterile environment, free from the messy, unpredictable influence of too many voices, including ours. The lease framework was largely in place before my team was even brought to the table.

"Well, of course," conventional real estate wisdom goes. "You're the architect, not a broker. Your job comes later." But this approach is rooted in fear.

The typical brokerage transaction team believes that outcomes will be worse if the design team gets involved too early. There is a deep-seated misconception that design thinking will derail the deal. They envision a Pandora's box of chaos opening before their eyes: the process will become unwieldy, employees will make outrageous and expensive demands, and the carefully negotiated terms will unravel. This fear is a powerful gatekeeper, preserving the linear, top-down process so embedded in commercial real estate, a process that feels safe and predictable. This process prioritizes the transaction over the transformation, the deal over the people.

This fear factor is magnified exponentially when the transaction team is exposed to the idea of Design Democracy for the first time. The very idea seems counterintuitive. How can the opinions of hundreds, or even thousands, of employees possibly contribute to a better, more efficient transaction? With the immense pressure of timing and the financial stakes involved, they are even less likely to risk opening the floodgates of company-wide feedback. It feels like an invitation for anarchy at the worst possible moment.

In the deal the broker and I were "tangoing" together, this fear of the Design Democracy process manifested in a seemingly generous offer from the landlord. As part of the lease agreement, they would include the cost of architecture and construction. This is a common tactic, a turnkey solution meant to simplify the process for the tenant. In reality, though, it's a mechanism of control. The landlord chose the architecture firm, and they chose the most notoriously budget-conscious firm in the region. Their goal was not to create the best possible workplace for our client; it was to deliver a finished space at the lowest possible cost to themselves.

The result was a predictable disaster. The landlord's design team, armed with a superficial understanding of our client's needs, repeatedly claimed there wasn't enough space in the building they were so eager to lease. Their architects produced space plans that crammed desks together, ignored critical adjacencies, and failed to provide the very amenities that were essential to the client's culture and workflow. The deal was on the verge of collapse, not because of a lack of space but because of a lack of knowledge. The transaction team, in their effort to control the process and avoid complexity, had created a crisis.

We were brought in to fix it, and succeeded just before everything blew up. How? We'll get into that in successive chapters, but for now I want to address what could've been done, pre-crisis, had I known the importance of brokers and had the power to integrate them into teams the right way.

The Broker Challenge

For better or for worse, brokers are a key part of commercial real estate and the design process. For brokers, the stakes of the job are high and the barrier to entry is low. Unlike the law, medicine, or architecture, there is no education, no rigorous licensure requirement, and no apprenticeship period; anyone who wants to can jump right into the field and be called a broker the very next day. Unfortunately, cities across America are littered with the rushed and poorly planned consequences of greedy, get-rich-quick brokers.

Of course, there are also truly great and brilliant people in brokerage—a highly competitive, sales-oriented service that rewards relationships and market presence. The job, when done well, can foster just the right combination of client, architect, and site selection. I witnessed brilliant brokers in action when I worked at Studley [now Savills] from 2006 to 2011, and again at Newmark Knight Frank from 2013 to 2016. These brokers understood that strategic design planning was critical to getting the real estate transaction right, and that they needed to include it at the earliest stages of a deal. In fact, much of what became the backbone of Design Democracy I learned during my time at Studley and Newmark. But the brokers I worked with there were the exception, not the rule.

The brokerage model in the United States is usually set up in the following way: one brokerage firm exclusively represents an organization or company, while another brokerage firm exclusively represents a target location. This separation creates clarity in the market and a more organized process. The key problem is that these brokers only get paid if the deal is done. This singular "finish line payday" creates massive risk for them. As a result, they want to reduce any factors that can negatively influence their deals or slow down the process. Often, their guiding motive is to move things along as fast as possible. The design and legal teams, with their detailed considerations and concerns, are just the kind of influences that brokers often want to minimize, as they slow down the brokers' aggressive timelines and add complexity to closing. While there are a few design teams that unnecessarily complicate things to generate more fees, even the one-size-fits-all architects out there still add far more value to a deal than the cost of their involvement. The really successful brokers know this and don't bristle at our desire to diligently determine the right size and right type of space before closing the deal. These professionals know that the risk of bringing the design team into lease negotiations is far outweighed by the clients' lasting satisfaction and enhanced performance as a result of our considerations. These are the brokerage teams that truly reign supreme; they know the value architects bring to the table and include them early in the process.

Much of the time, however, you'll get teams that try to go it alone. They don't partner with other brokers, so they don't have to share commissions, and they certainly don't choose to bring architects in early. Occasionally, a brokerage team will be eager to use the Design Democracy magic, but because the field is so used to overlooking the input of architects, they don't know when to engage with us. We've seen it dozens of times. Rookie teams reach out to us for help with next steps during the site selection process. Our new clients and these brokers often tell us that they've already interviewed company leadership, filled out programming documentation, and even done some surveys. They are so proud of themselves. But they're often looking at the wrong things and are three steps ahead of where they need to be, which means they'll have to backtrack for the real Design Democracy process to work.

It gets a little sticky at this point, because the first thing we often have to tell these brokers and our mutual client is that they have some of the basics wrong; they are looking at the wrong size and type of space, and we have to carefully reverse these broker-performed designs because they lack the necessary scale of participation, depth of inquiry, and structured use of data to truly inform the design.

Design Democracy forms the foundation of the transaction and resulting design process; it isn't an add-on feature to include at the end. So, we work backwards with these clients and brokerage teams to ensure the three pillars of Design Democracy are in place before continuing.

The Three Pillars of Design Democracy

As we've covered in previous chapters, the traditional approach to workplace design is a top-down affair. A handful of executives, perhaps with the input of a few department heads, make decisions that will impact the daily lives of hundreds, if not thousands, of employees. This process is both efficient and deeply flawed because it's based on the assumption that a small group of people understand the complex, nuanced needs of their diverse workforce.

Design Democracy is a radical departure from this model; it's built on the belief that the people who use a space are the true experts on how that space should function. Its methodology is designed to be inclusive, data-driven, and, above all, effective.

There are three core pillars of Design Democracy: scale of participation, depth of inquiry, and the structured use of data. Without any one of these pillars, the structure of Design Democracy won't hold, and the benefits of the process won't be nearly as profound. Let's go through each pillar in more detail—what it is, why it's so important in the design process, and how its effects can be felt across an organization.

Pillar One: Scale of Participation

The scale of participation is the first and most important pillar of the Design Democracy process. Instead of relying on the opinions of a select few, we invite every single member of an organization to participate in the design process. Our goal is to create a chorus of voices, a rich and diverse tapestry of perspectives that will inform every decision we make.

We typically see a response rate of around sixty percent, a number that testifies to the power of this inclusive approach. People are eager to share their thoughts, have their voices heard, and be a part of something that will have a direct impact on their daily lives. And the impact of this participation goes far beyond the data we collect, creating a sense of ownership throughout the organization.

The simple act of asking is a powerful thing. It communicates respect and the recognition that every individual's experience and perspective has value. This is true even for those who choose not to participate in the design process. Simply knowing that they had the opportunity to do so, that their voice mattered enough to be solicited, is often enough to create that sense of buy-in and satisfaction in the end result.

And that end result is a workplace designed not just for the people but by the people—a space that reflects the collective wisdom of the organization, that expresses its true culture and values, and where people feel a sense of belonging, a sense of pride, and a sense of ownership.

Pillar Two: Depth of Inquiry

The second pillar of Design Democracy is our depth of inquiry. It's not enough to simply ask people what they want. We need to ask them the right questions, in the right way, to get to the heart of what truly matters to them. Our engagement process needs to be both comprehensive and efficient; think of it like a deep dive into the needs and desires of the organization, but one that still keeps people's attention. Aim for a survey that takes no longer than thirty minutes.

Include a mix of narrative and visual questions, a combination that allows us to tap into both the analytical and the intuitive sides of the brain. Narrative questions allow space for people to communicate the stories of their daily work lives. Visual questions, on the other hand, allow participants to explore more abstract concepts, to get a feel for the aesthetic and atmospheric qualities that will make the space feel right.

All of the questions should be multiple choice, a format that is both easy to answer and easy to analyze. And be sure to randomize the order of the questions so that every question gets equal engagement, even from those who don't complete the entire survey. Additionally, ask the same question in different ways, a technique that allows you to cross-reference the data and identify any inconsistencies.

The result of this depth of inquiry is a rich and detailed picture of an organization's needs and a deep understanding of the what, the why, and the how of employees' work—the foundation of a truly effective workplace design.

Pillar Three: Structured Use of Data

The third and final pillar of Design Democracy is the structured use of data. In a world that is increasingly data-driven, it's remarkable how many major business decisions are still based on gut feelings and anecdotal evidence. The design of a workplace is no exception to this tendency. All too often, the opinions of a few powerful individuals drown out the voices of the many, leading to a design that reflects personal preferences over organizational needs.

Time and time again, people who thought they knew better than the data have been proven wrong. When we've compared the initial ideas of leadership with the data-driven insights of our process, the two have been different in every single case. This is not to say that leadership is always wrong, but it is to say that their perspective is naturally limited.

The Design Democracy process corrects this course by collecting a massive amount of data and turning it into actionable insights. We look for patterns, areas of consensus, and pools of disagreement. We create a clear and compelling narrative, grounded in the data and impossible to ignore.

This data becomes the ultimate arbiter, the final authority on what an organization truly needs. Its structured use is a powerful tool for building consensus, aligning stakeholders, and making design decisions in the best interests of the whole organization. This pillar depoliticizes the design process by moving it from the realm of personal opinion to the realm of objective fact.

Recommendations for Leaders Who Want a Design-Led Transaction

The traditional real estate process is broken. It prioritizes the transaction over the transformation, the deal over the people. But it doesn't have to be this way. By embracing Design Democracy, you can take control of your real estate project and create a workplace that truly reflects your organization's culture and values. Here are a few key recommendations to get you started:

1. *Choose a broker after you choose an architect.*
   This may seem counterintuitive, but it's the single most important thing you can do to ensure a design-led approach. By choosing your architect first, you are sending a clear message that design is your top priority. You are putting the focus on the transformation, not the transaction. And you are empowering your design team to take the lead in the process, to be your advocate and your guide.

2. *If you already have a broker, insist that they involve an architect immediately.*
   If you are already in a relationship with a broker, it's not too late to change the dynamic. Insist that they bring an architect to the table immediately, and that the architect has full visibility into the transaction. This is common practice for mid- to large-sized organizations with multiple locations, and the model can be adapted to any project.

3. *Interview your team.*

   The success of your project will depend on the quality of your team. Take time to interview the people you are considering for your brokerage and design teams. Make sure they thoroughly understand the concept of Design Democracy. If you're not hearing ideas that sound like the collaborative, empathy-based ones you're hearing in this book, you might be with the wrong people.

The future of work is not, as overnight brokers might have us believe, about cramming as many people as possible into the smallest possible space, nor is it about finishing a project as soon as possible. It's about creating environments that support the way people actually work and spaces that inspire. It's about creating a workplace that functions as a competitive advantage for attracting and retaining the best talent. And it's about creating a space that reflects your organization's culture and values. This is the promise of Design Democracy, and it's a promise within reach.

Chapter 6:

Patterns of Life

I'm not someone who puts a lot of weight in trends. In the world of design and architecture, trends are seductive but ultimately hollow. They are the averages, the smoothed-over distillations of what's popular at any given moment. To design by trend is to design for the mean, and in doing so, to ignore the beautiful, messy, and essential details of individuals and the nuanced differences between cultures of even similar companies. It's a statistical shortcut that sacrifices specificity for style.

I started to question the value of trends the first time a client asked me to design them an office like Google's. This was years ago, and Google's new campuses, with their open-concept plans and playful amenities, were the talk of the industry. The leadership team from this internet-based accounting startup insisted they were "just like Google" and wanted all the same cool stuff: a fire pole, a slide, several Ping-Pong tables. This is a classic example of preference falsification on an organizational scale—a company mistaking a popular trend for its own authentic identity. I hadn't fully developed Design Democracy yet, but my intuition told me that running a design on trend alone was a direct path to failure.

So, in those early days, we started by simply asking a lot of questions. We administered a slow, manual, in-person version of our survey, asking things like, "Do you work in groups or alone?" and "What are the primary functions performed in this space?" We talked to as many people as we could. The data quickly revealed the truth: they were an accounting firm first and a tech firm second. Their culture was dominated by the need for quiet, focused work. No one was interested in a fire pole, and as much as I love Ping-Pong, trying to do your taxes next to a game is a recipe for disaster.

The silver lining was that the founder was a true leader; he had no problem confronting the fear of being wrong. When we presented our report, two things happened. First, he immediately let go of the fire pole and the slide. Second, because our deep dive had revealed their authentic cultural needs, it became clear that they would benefit from a large, café-style event space in place of a traditional reception area. That's what we built: a space with an abundance of private, quiet zones, anchored by a big, open kitchen and café that became the heart of their company. The final space was innovative because it reflected *their* culture, creating a new pattern that was just for them, completely different from any trend.

No two law firms are the same. No two technology companies are the same. Even if these companies have similar goals, operate in the same city, and compete for the same talent, they have different people and thus have different cultures. To apply a single design trend—the industrial-chic open plan, the minimalist Scandinavian aesthetic, the playful tech-campus vibe—to all of them is to fundamentally misunderstand what makes an organization tick. That would be like giving every person the same size T-shirt and expecting it to be a perfect fit.

While I'm deeply cautious about trends, I am a devout student of patterns. When design really works, when it creates a place that feels not just new but *right*, it is the result of deep listening and the inclusion of timeless patterns.

Patterns are not averages. Averages smooth out variation, erasing the peaks and valleys of human need. Patterns, in contrast, are recurring solutions to recurring problems. Patterns highlight something fundamental about how we live and work. They are principles that guide us, not prescriptions we must follow. Areas and materials that nurture our physical comfort, our human interactions, and our systems of self-care are common focal points that appear across time and in all types of built environments. These patterns are the threads of a universal language.

Architect and design theorist Christopher Alexander dedicated his life to articulating this idea. In *The Timeless Way of Building*, he describes a profound, often intangible quality that separates living, whole spaces from dead, fragmented ones. He called it the "Quality Without a Name." The feeling of a sun-drenched window seat, the comfortable buzz of a neighborhood café, the quiet dignity of a well-crafted wooden door—these encapsulate that feeling of being alive, whole, and connected to a place.

Alexander argued that we don't achieve this quality by following architectural fads or imposing a rigid, top-down master plan on a project. We achieve it by using a shared *pattern language*. A pattern language is a network of both the recurring problems we face as humans and the recurring solutions we find. Because our problems are similar, so are the core solutions to those problems; we can use these solutions a million times over, without ever doing them the same way twice.

Patterns give us a common vocabulary to design and build spaces that are truly alive. This chapter is about identifying those core patterns for the modern workplace so that each of our designs uniquely solves the common problems we face in our workplaces today.

The Intuition We All Share

You don't need an architecture degree to recognize that "Quality Without a Name." There is a deep, common ground in what people like and don't like about the spaces we inhabit. It's not always a matter of subjective personal taste. Everyone likes windows. Everyone prefers a comfortable chair to a hard one. Everyone feels better in a clean, well-lit room than in a dark, dingy one.

We all know what bad looks like; we've all been in those spaces. Think of the soul-crushing DMV waiting room with its humming fluorescent lights, sticky linoleum floors, and rows of bolted-down plastic chairs. Think of the windowless basement office, the cramped airplane seat, the noisy restaurant where you have to shout to be heard. We recognize these places as fundamentally broken. They lack the "Quality Without a Name." They are dead spaces that drain our energy and make us feel small.

The challenge is that while we can easily identify "bad," we can't always picture what "good" looks like, especially in the context of our own work. We are so accustomed to compromise that we often fail to imagine something better. This is where a pattern language becomes so powerful. It gives us the tools to articulate not just what's wrong but how to make it right. It helps us see that certain elements work in almost any environment because they solve fundamental human problems. By breaking down the complexity of a workplace into a series of core patterns, we can begin building a shared vision for a space that's both functional and alive.

Let's explore three of the most critical patterns that form the foundation of any great workplace: physical comfort, human interaction, and self-care. A workplace must provide, foster, and support all three of these patterns to possess that "Quality Without a Name."

Pattern 1: Physical Comfort

The Problem: Human beings are physical creatures, not disembodied minds floating around in a digital cloud. To do our best work, to think clearly, and to collaborate effectively, our bodies must be at ease. Physical discomfort—whether from a bad chair, poor lighting, or stale air—is a constant, low-level tax on our attention. These persistent distractions slowly but surely drain our cognitive resources, sap away our motivation, and degrade our well-being. A workplace that ignores the physical comfort of its people is a workplace that is fundamentally inefficient and inhumane.

The Solution: Create an environment that actively nurtures the body by providing high-quality, ergonomic tools, access to natural elements like light and fresh air, and a significant degree of personal choice and control within each person's immediate surroundings.

There are a few ways to create this baseline of physical well-being:

Include natural light.

Including natural light in your designs is perhaps the most powerful and least expensive tool in the designer's arsenal. Access to daylight and views of the outdoors is not a perk; it is a biological necessity. Sunlight helps regulate our circadian rhythms, which control our sleep-wake cycles and impact everything from mood to hormone production. Studies have consistently shown that workers in environments with ample natural light report less eye strain, fewer headaches, and higher levels of energy and productivity.

Windows connect us to the rhythm of a day and the changing of the seasons. They're not mere apertures framing a great view. By placing open areas and pathways along window walls and using glass for interior partitions, you can design a space that prioritizes daylight, the first and most important step in creating a comfortable environment.

Ensure access to fresh air and high air quality.

What we breathe is as important as what we see. Too often, modern office buildings function like a sealed box, recirculating air that becomes laden with carbon dioxide, volatile organic compounds (VOCs) from carpets and furniture, and other pollutants. The result is a stale, stuffy environment that leads to drowsiness, difficulty concentrating, and what is often called "sick building syndrome."

The solution is simple in principle: bring in more fresh air. This can be achieved through advanced heating, ventilation, and air conditioning (HVAC) systems with high-grade filtration, but the most timeless and effective method is the operable window. The simple act of opening a window to let in a breeze is a profound act of empowerment, as it gives individuals control over the quality of the air they breathe.

Provide ergonomic task chairs.

If the knowledge worker has one essential tool, it is their chair. We spend thousands of hours sitting per year, and a poorly designed chair can cause chronic back pain, neck strain, and a host of other musculoskeletal problems. A high-quality, ergonomic task chair solves the issue. Decades of research have gone into creating chairs that provide proper lumbar support, adjust to a wide range of body types, and move with the user. Providing these chairs for every employee is not an indulgence; it is a fundamental investment in their health and productivity. It is one of the most direct ways a company can say, "We care about your physical well-being."

Give employees personal control.
> Perhaps the most critical element of physical comfort is a sense of personal control. Everyone is different. Some people run hot, others run cold. Some prefer bright light for focused work, while others need a dimmer environment. A one-size-fits-all approach is doomed to fail. A great workplace gives people agency over their immediate environment. This includes a variety of seating options and/or sit-stand desks that allow users to change their posture throughout the day, as well as task lighting that can be individually adjusted. When we lack control, we feel stress. When we have control, we feel comfortable and respected.

Pattern 2: Human Interaction

The Problem: Work is, and always has been, a social activity. We come together to share ideas, solve problems, build relationships, and create things we could not create alone. Our physical environment can either be a catalyst for this interaction or a major impediment. Spaces that are too loud or too formal, or spaces that lack the right tools, can stifle collaboration. On the other hand, a complete lack of privacy can also make meaningful connection impossible.

The Solution: A single, cavernous open-plan office or a monolithic block of identical conference rooms fails to recognize the varied nature of collaboration. Design a diverse ecosystem of spaces that support the full spectrum of human interaction, from private, focused conversations to large, energetic gatherings, all supported by seamlessly embedded and frictionless technology.

Design a living workplace with a rich tapestry of settings by including some or all of the following elements:

A spectrum of meeting spaces

A modern workplace needs a variety of meeting spaces. This includes small, two-to-four-person "huddle rooms" for quick check-ins and private conversations; medium-sized, six-to-eight-person rooms for team meetings and presentations; and larger, flexible spaces that can be reconfigured for workshops or all-hands gatherings. Crucially, creating meeting spaces means accounting for informal meeting areas too—clusters of comfortable chairs in an open area, booths in a café, or benches in a wide corridor. These encourage the serendipitous, unplanned conversations where so much innovation is born.

The reception-adjacent, twenty-person boardroom is an artifact of a bygone era. While still occasionally useful, it is a highly inefficient use of space for the majority of daily interactions. It dominates the highest-traffic part of the space with the lowest-frequency use, and, when it *is* used, privacy is almost always paramount. People don't usually want to be seen meeting in these rooms, or heard. Consider excluding this traditional meeting space in favor of more multi-purpose spaces that accommodate a variety of needs and roles.

Frictionless, embedded technology

In a world of hybrid work, technology is the connective tissue that binds teams together. But too often, it is a source of profound frustration. The five minutes wasted at the beginning of every meeting trying to connect a laptop to the screen or get the video conference audio to work is a tax on productivity and morale. Technology should be an invisible enabler, not a constant obstacle. This means investing in systems that are simple, reliable, and standardized across all meeting spaces. It means large, high-resolution screens, high-quality cameras and microphones, and simple, one-touch connectivity. Make power outlets abundant and easily accessible everywhere, not just in conference rooms. And a strong, reliable Wi-Fi signal should be as ubiquitous as the air itself. The goal of investing in high-quality technology is to make collaborating with a colleague on another continent feel as natural as talking to the person sitting next to you.

Acoustic comfort

The success of any collaborative environment, especially one with open-plan elements, hinges on acoustics. A constant barrage of noise from neighboring conversations, phone calls, and foot traffic is a major source of distraction and stress. Good acoustic design means crafting sound into zones with varied acoustic properties, not ensuring total silence throughout the workplace. This zone creation involves sound-absorbing materials like acoustic ceiling tiles, carpets, and fabric-wrapped panels. It also means creating "neighborhoods" with either physical or perceived boundaries to contain noise. And it means providing ample, easily accessible quiet zones—like phone booths, focus areas, and small, enclosed rooms—where people can retreat for concentrated work or private conversations.

Pattern 3: Self-Care

The Problem: People are holistic, no matter how much we try to separate our work lives from our private lives or achieve that delicate work-life balance. We have basic human needs for nourishment, rest, and restoration that must be met throughout the day. A workplace that treats these needs as an afterthought—say, providing a depressing, dirty breakroom or subpar restrooms—sends a clear and demoralizing message: your personal well-being is not our priority. This neglect leads to burnout, disengagement, and a feeling of being devalued.

The Solution: Design and maintain high-quality, restorative, and dignified spaces that support personal well-being and signal a deep, institutional respect for workers as human beings.

The following spaces are often considered "soft" amenities, but they are, in fact, critical infrastructure for a healthy and high-performing culture:

The office café as the hearth

The traditional breakroom is dead. In its place is the office café, a place to get coffee and the social heart of a workplace. This is the modern-day hearth or village well, the central gathering place where people from different teams and hierarchies can connect in a relaxed, informal setting. A great café can include a fancy espresso machine, but far more than that, it should provide high-quality, healthy, and appealing food and beverage options for a variety of tastes. The overarching idea of this space is to create a comfortable and inviting atmosphere with multiple seating options and good lighting. Aim for a welcoming ambiance to encourage chance encounters or solo mental breaks to recharge. Investing in a great café is a direct investment in both individual well-being and the social fabric and collective energy of an organization.

The dignity of the restroom

No space reveals a company's true attitude toward its employees more than its restrooms. It is the most private space in a public building, and its design has a profound psychological impact. A poorly maintained, dimly lit, or cramped restroom is a daily indignity that communicates a fundamental lack of care and respect. A clean, bright, and well-designed restroom communicates the opposite; it is a sign that an organization cares for and deeply respects its employees. Achieving this means providing full-length doors on stalls for privacy, good lighting for grooming, high-quality, reliable fixtures, and thoughtful touches like touchless faucets and ample counter space. It means ensuring the space is always clean and well-stocked. Well-designed, consistently maintained bathrooms are nonnegotiable if the goal is creating a workplace where people feel valued and cared for.

The Living Language of Work

These three patterns, physical comfort, human interaction, and self-care, are not a checklist to be ticked off nor an afterthought. They are foundational elements if you want to design a living workplace that encapsulates the "Quality Without a Name." These patterns are also interconnected and mutually reinforcing. A comfortable chair is of little use in a room with no fresh air. A great meeting room is useless if the technology is impossible to use. A beautiful café will sit empty if people are too stressed and uncomfortable at their desks to leave them.

The goal is to weave these patterns together, to move beyond the fleeting whims of trends into the timeless, universal needs of people. This process requires leaders and designers to stop thinking in terms of averages and start listening for patterns. Human needs are never smooth, but designing for their basic dignity doesn't mean you have to reinvent the wheel. All it takes is recognizing our shared language: that intuition we all have for what makes a place feel right, what makes a place feel *alive*.

If that is your aim and your focus, you will design far more than a building. You will create an environment that speaks a living language, a place that is flexible, adaptable, and deeply attuned to the human beings within it. Speaking this language, embedding it into every design consideration, negotiation, and drawing, is a strategic asset. You will become known for creating spaces that foster well-being, enhance collaboration, and physically manifest a company's best self. You will move beyond designing places where people *have* to be to places where people *want* to be. That is the power of patterns.

Chapter 7:

Culture Over Tradition

I've worked with so many people who call themselves workplace strategists. Very few of them are. For years, I've observed a fundamental rift in the field, a divide that separates the truly transformative strategists from the merely trendy ones who throw around the term without anything to show for it.

On one side, you have the genuine strategists, nearly all of whom have a design background. This doesn't mean they're inherently more creative, but it generally means their approach to workplace strategy is rooted in empathy. These corporate ethnographers and design thinkers lean into listening not just to hear requests but to record the subtle, critical differences from one organization to another, studying groups to understand the intricate flow of human interaction defining an organization. They try to get at the essence of workflow, the unwritten rules of engagement, and the day-to-day culture that makes a company unique. They know that the soul of a company isn't found in its mission statement; it's in the coffee-stained cafe conversations and the energy of a project team deep in flow.

Then there is the other group, who, unfortunately, call themselves by the same name. These not-so-helpful workplace strategists are far more common and, frankly, a dangerous breed. They hail from varied non-design backgrounds, like finance, data science, economics, or commercial real estate—and they bring the tools of their trade to a problem that cannot be solved by their tools alone. Their objective is to spread the reassuringly bland paste of averages into the nuanced practice of calculating and creating space. Sometimes it's the youngest member of a brokerage team, a wizard with spreadsheets, who has been tasked with calculating a company's spatial needs. He opens his Excel model, plugs in the headcount, applies an industry-standard square-foot-per-person metric from a three-year-old market report, and spits out a number. The number is precise, defensible, and utterly devoid of humanity.

Sometimes it's the newly minted data scientist, armed with terabytes of information, who confidently proclaims that the average of all "creative office space" is the future of *your* creative office. Incorrect. Don't get me wrong, these are very smart people, people who excelled in disciplines built on logic and quantitative analysis. But they are trying to apply the blunt instrument of averages to the delicate, complex measure of human experience. Their process is seductive in its simplicity. They count up the people, multiply this by the assumed size of workstations and offices, and then sprinkle in some generalized assumptions about conference rooms based on industry benchmarks. Then, *voilà!* They have a program for a new office, perfectly average and perfectly soulless, but perfectly able to get client approval, nonetheless. It never ends up being quite right—the space is often loud where it should be quiet, distant where it should be connected—but it *looks* cool. Someone takes pretty pictures for the corporate website and the architectural magazines, so no one complains. The critical follow-up study to calculate if the new space actually accomplished its true goals—to increase collaboration, foster innovation, or improve well-being—rarely, if ever, takes place.

I'm rough on this second group, because in recent years they have taken a disproportionately large role in the needs analysis and design development aspects of a new project, things that were almost exclusively the job of architects and designers. While it's true that calculating the amount of space needed is a combination of data collection and information analytics, and while it's a vital part of the design process that belongs in a lease and has significant financial implications, this process shouldn't be developed solely by the leasing team or a bunch of data futurists who are looking at the problem from 30,000 feet. Design, especially Design Democracy, requires both the long view and the face-to-face conversations with those who will actually inhabit the spaces we create.

Technology, when used correctly, can be our greatest ally. Artificial intelligence is already making powerful recommendations, but it's doing this by helping us uncover and visualize complex patterns pulled from real interactions with individuals, not by calculating and spitting out broad averages. It's a scalpel, not a sledgehammer, and those who wield it need to approach these decisions with equal precision.

The High Cost of Empty Chairs

The abstract nature of poor design strategy often allows it to fly under the radar of corporate leadership. But people start to listen, and listen very carefully, when you put a dollar value on the space they are not using.

In the world of workplace design, we consider eighty percent occupancy at any given time to be about full occupancy of a dynamic, healthy organization. This twenty percent buffer accounts for the normal rhythms of work life: people are out at client meetings, traveling for business, home with a sick child, on maternity leave, or simply out for lunch. So, if your state-of-the-art, beautifully designed headquarters is consistently running at forty percent peak occupancy, a number that became shockingly common post-pandemic, you are effectively paying for a space double the size you actually need. Half of your space is being wasted.

Let's translate that into concrete terms. Say you're a mid-sized company paying $250,000 per month in rent, a perfectly normal figure for 60,000 square feet in a major market like Los Angeles or New York. If your occupancy data shows you're only using half of that space, then you are flushing approximately $125,000 down the toilet every single month.

Even the most stoic CFO will sit up straight when you tell them they are burning $1.5 million a year on wasted rent. That's not a line item; that's a crisis. That's the budget for an entire R&D team. It's a marketing campaign that never launches. It's a dozen new hires you can't afford to make. And this calculation only scratches the surface. It doesn't account for the associated operational costs of that empty space, the utilities, the maintenance, the taxes. Nor does it capture the immense, hidden cost of a disengaged workforce rattling around in a space that feels like a ghost town.

Suddenly, "workplace strategy" is no longer a soft, HR-led initiative; it's a core financial imperative.

Siren Song of the Status Quo

In the early aughts, after the first internet bubble burst and reformed, it was clear the digital revolution would continue to reshape not just business models but entire company cultures. In this new landscape, Google became the North Star for the design community. They turned the traditional, hierarchical office layout on its head. The coveted corner offices, once the ultimate symbol of corporate power, were largely eliminated. In their place, Google created a dynamic ecosystem of spaces: bustling micro-kitchens designed to spark "creative collisions," cafés that doubled as workstations, and an abundance of indoor-outdoor space that blurred the lines between work and life. While many of these innovations positively influenced modern design, they are not, and were never intended to be, a one-size-fits-all solution.

The problem was, we as a design community were now faced with a flood of new companies—and old companies desperate to feel new—that all wanted to be "just like Google." They saw the playful aesthetic, the free food, and the vibrant colors, and they wanted to copy and paste it onto their own organizations. The issue, of course, was that these firms were not Google. Their logic was flawed. Companies copied the artifacts of Google's culture without understanding the principles that created it. After all, the tailored suit that looks impeccable on one person can look ridiculous and ill-fitting on another, and the same thing is true in design.

Nevertheless, the open office plan became everyone's future, whether it fit an organization or not. Seemingly overnight, every company, from law firms to insurance agencies, felt they needed a wide-open floor plan, complete with a beer keg and kombucha on tap.. But these new trends were profoundly misunderstood. The innovations that worked for Google were diluted, stripped of their original purpose, and repackaged as shorthand gimmicks. They became tools to attract talent in a competitive market while simultaneously, and conveniently, stuffing more people into less space. Fostering a specific company culture got lost between these new and endless rows of workstations.

To be true to a company's culture, the space must be authentic. Even in those early days of the changing office environment, I was sure that not every organization needed the same solution. A team of software engineers requires long periods of deep, uninterrupted focus; forcing them into a loud, open environment is an act of managerial malpractice. Not every company would benefit from having a Ping-Pong table in their office. Have you ever tried to write three coherent sentences of an important email near someone playing a spirited game of Ping-Pong? It's nearly impossible. The noise, the movement, the sheer kinetic energy are distracting by design.

By 2012, I had developed an early version of the Design Democracy platform and was using it on just about every project. It found its first champions in technology companies, not because the platform was flashy but because they understood and appreciated its purpose. They liked its technology-based due diligence; it was the only way to determine *their* specific needs—just the right amount of space for meeting, for private solo work, for frequent events, and, yes, to determine if they were the right kind of company for a Ping-Pong table. When Design Democracy was involved, even in its nascent stages, the results were clear and immediate: companies experienced better engagement in the space, higher employee satisfaction, and more consistent attendance.

The Designer's Dilemma

A project can only be as authentic as the designer allows it to be. And here we encounter one of the deepest, most pervasive fears within the creative professions: the fear of not having singular ownership of a project. This fear is a core component of *impostor syndrome*, that nagging, persistent feeling that you're a fraud who's about to be called out, who doesn't truly deserve the credit for your successes.

When you invite a client, not to mention an entire organization, into the creative process, you are ceding a degree of creative control. Some designers report feeling like mere functionaries when they share the genesis of a design with their clients. By co-creating with the very people who will inhabit the space, they feel like importers, assembling a collection of preferences rather than creating a singular, cohesive vision. But beneath this feeling lies the deep-down fear that they don't deserve success if they share it with others. This fear pushes designers toward the safety of the known. A trend, after all, is a pre-validated choice. It's harder for a client to argue with "This is the aesthetic that's winning awards right now" than it is to defend a unique solution derived from a messy, collaborative process.

Impostor syndrome loves it when we compare ourselves to others. We look at our own chaotic, behind-the-scenes work—all the wrong turns, the moments of self-doubt, the last-minute changes—and we compare it to someone else's shiny, finished product. We compare our blooper reel to their highlight reel. It's a game we can never win.

In the design world, this anxiety is cranked up to eleven by portfolio sites like Pinterest and Instagram. When we scroll through endless feeds of pixel-perfect designs and flawless case studies, it's so easy to feel like our own work, with all its real-world problems, budget compromises, and stakeholder concessions, just doesn't measure up.

This pressure creates a powerful incentive to present a clean, linear narrative of genius, where the designer bestows a brilliant vision upon a grateful client. But the truth is always messier and more interesting. No two people or two companies are exactly the same. The company culture and the way work actually gets done should be the sole drivers of design decisions, not the underlying fear of being an imposter. Design will inevitably miss the mark when the designer is far removed from the end user, overlaying picture-perfect designs onto messy realities, or when a company is trying to emulate a design that doesn't suit its culture or way of working.

The Perils of Chasing Trends

Trends are not inherently evil. They can be helpful as an early source of comfort and idea creation. They provide a starting point, a common language, and a visual library of what's possible. But the comfort of a trend can quickly become a cage. The moment a design choice is justified with "it's what everyone is doing" is the moment authenticity begins to die. Remember, what's right for someone else might not be right for you, even if you're in the same industry and the same city. Even if it looks good to you.

A successful law firm in downtown Los Angeles might thrive in a sleek, modern space with glass-walled offices and a minimalist aesthetic that communicates precision and stability. But that same design could feel cold, sterile, and creatively stifling to a scrappy advertising agency just a few blocks away. The legal team may value the quiet dignity and acoustic privacy of a traditional office, which allows for confidential client calls and focused document review. The ad agency, on the other hand, might need a space that buzzes with energy, with open project zones, writable walls, and flexible furniture that can be reconfigured for brainstorming sessions and client pitches. One design isn't inherently better than the other, but each space must be an authentic reflection of the unique culture it houses. To impose the law firm's aesthetic on the ad agency would be to fundamentally misunderstand and undermine their work.

The Power of Listening

The antidote to the tyranny of trends is simple, though not always easy: listening. True listening is not a passive act of recording requests. It is an active, engaged, and structured process of seeking to understand. Crucially, it's not about trying to please everyone. That's a fool's errand that leads to a muddled, compromised design that satisfies no one. The goal of listening to everyone is to identify and develop patterns from what you hear. People are smarter than we give them credit for. Everyone understands that they can't always get what they want, and they will be surprisingly satisfied with the outcome if they feel genuinely heard and respected throughout the process.

This is the essence of Design Democracy. It's not about giving every employee a vote on the color of the walls or the style of the chairs. It's about creating a robust, transparent process where every voice has value, where every perspective is considered, and where the final design is a synthesis of an organization's collective wisdom.

Think of this design process as a way to understand the culture better. At the simplest level, even for a fairly straightforward project, we use a visual online survey and a narrative online survey. (Please refer to Appendix G for examples of these surveys.)

When you use consensus-building technology and techniques to identify the unique elements of each company and the way work gets done there, you are doing more than just programming a building. When you ask people what they need to do their best work, you are not just gathering data for a floor plan; you are taking a high-resolution snapshot of an organization's soul. You are learning about its communication styles, hidden workflows, core values, and collective aspirations. The design process thus becomes a mirror, reflecting the organization back to itself and revealing truths that were previously hidden in plain sight.

Data-Driven Authenticity

When you have this rich, cultural data, you are no longer guessing at solutions. You are not relying on trends, averages, or the subjective opinions of a few powerful people in the C-suite to design a workplace for an entire company. You have the cultural data to make bold, authentic choices that are easily justifiable because they are data-based.

This data becomes both your guide and your shield. When a senior executive insists on a private corner office out of tradition, you can point to sociometric data and network graphs showing that the people they collaborate with most are located on the other side of the building, and that a more central, accessible office would dramatically improve the communication flow between them. When a department head lobbies for a large, open-plan workplace because they believe it fosters collaboration, you can show them survey results and observational data indicating a desperate need for quiet, focused work areas and propose a "library" zone instead.

The data you gather through the Design Democracy process brings fairness to the design process, transforming it from a battle of strong wills and personal opinions into a collaborative search for the most effective solution for all. It provides cover for both the designer and the client to make the right choice, not just the easiest or most politically expedient one. This isn't about "Big Data" in the abstract sense; it's about "Thick Data," the qualitative, contextual information that reveals the *why* behind the numbers. It's the stories, the frustrations, and the ideas of the people themselves that give meaning to your quantitative data.

In the next chapter, we'll explore how to take this authentic, data-driven vision and align it with the hard realities of financial constraints and measurable business outcomes. But the foundation of any successful design project is this unwavering commitment to authenticity. It's about having the courage to reject the easy answers, to listen deeply to people's needs, and to create a space that reflects a company's true culture.

Chapter 8:

Design for Real Life

If the office is going to be a place of empowerment, it must reflect the deepest ethos of the group it aims to empower.

How many times have you had lunch in a windowless breakroom? How many times have you wrestled with conference room technology that's in the wrong place or simply broken? We've all had these experiences, and we don't spend any more time in those spaces than we have to. On the way out of that breakroom, it's all too common to walk past private offices with million-dollar views or beautiful, glass-walled conference rooms with state-of-the-art technology—and no one in them. They are sitting unused, designed for a world that no longer exists.

How did we get here? The transition from endless rows of desks and 9-to-5 attendance to the freedom of a hybrid schedule and a flexible workplace is no accident, and the design of our workplaces has always reflected this push and pull. But to understand this trajectory, we have to go back to the rise of the "information worker" and our journey from human calculators to creative collaborators.

The Information Factory

Let's jump back to the early 1900s. Big companies were getting bigger, and they needed a new kind of employee: the clerical worker. These were the original information workers, armed with typewriters, tabulation machines, and filing cabinets, whose job was to process mountains of paperwork. Their work, while brain-powered, was incredibly repetitive, much like an assembly line.

So, naturally, the first real offices were designed like factories. An efficiency guru named Frederick Winslow Taylor had a big idea called "scientific management," which was actually quite simple: find the best way to do a task and make everyone do it exactly that way, no variation. This concept, when applied to office design, created the classic open-plan layout. Think of Frank Lloyd Wright's Larkin Building from 1906 as an example of this, a huge, open room with desks lined up in perfect, grid-like rows.

This period in our working history, and how it was reflected in workplace design, was all about efficiency and control. Bosses got private offices, often on a higher floor or a mezzanine, so they could literally look down on their workforce. The straight desk rows made it easy to pass paperwork from one station to the next, just like parts moving along a conveyor belt. These spaces didn't intend to foster creative thinking; they were "information factories," built to process data quickly and keep everyone in line and on task.

The Rise of the Knowledge Worker

After World War II, the corporate world got a lot more complicated. Work itself changed on a broad scale, and a new type of employee emerged, one that management expert Peter Drucker famously termed the "knowledge worker." The knowledge worker was someone who didn't just push information around but created it, analyzing problems, brainstorming ideas, and making complex decisions.

Suddenly, the rigid, factory-style office didn't make sense anymore. This new kind of work demanded flexibility, collaboration, and a bit of privacy for deep thought. The old model was failing, which led to some fascinating experiments in office design.

One of the most radical was a German concept from the 1950s called "Burolandschaft," or "office landscape." These designers threw out the grid, arranged desks into organic clusters, and used plants as natural dividers to make the layout feel more natural and encourage collaboration. Treating employees like a community instead of cogs in a machine was a revolutionary idea at the time.

Meanwhile, in the US, a designer named Robert Propst came up with the "Action Office," a brilliant modular system of movable walls, desks, and shelves. His design came from a simple observation during his time at Herman Miller: people didn't work on one thing all day, so they shouldn't have to be in the same setting all day either. Think of Propst's layout like an office LEGO set; companies could create unique, flexible workplaces tailored to their teams at any time, depending on their need and the task at hand.

It was a novel concept, and a potentially useful one. But then, corporations did what they often do: they found a way to make it cheaper and more soul-crushing. Propst's vision of a flexible, empowering toolkit of movable pieces got stripped down into the thing we all love to hate: the cubicle. The modular walls became fixed, gray prisons, and the dream of a dynamic workplace turned into a sea of identical, isolating boxes. The cubicle farm was born, a sad compromise that offered the illusion of privacy without any of the real benefits of either an open office or a closed one. Propst himself would later call this a "monolithic insanity."

The Digital Revolution

The arrival of the personal computer in the '80s followed by the internet in the '90s completely changed the landscape of work. Information was no longer trapped in a filing cabinet; it was digital, instant, and accessible to anyone from anywhere, untethering the information worker once and for all.

This tech revolution blew up office design. At first, companies just stuffed bulky computers into their existing cubicles. But as tech got smaller and more mobile, it became clear the old ways wouldn't work. This led to a major comeback of the open-plan office, championed by the booming tech startups in Silicon Valley who believed that tearing down walls could spark "creative collisions" and foster rapid-fire innovation. The office became a place filled with shared tables, comfy lounge areas, and brainstorming rooms with wall-to-wall whiteboards. Workplace perks and company culture became a focal point as well. Companies like Google built sprawling campuses with free cafés, gyms, and volleyball courts. The office wasn't just a place to work anymore; it was a destination designed to attract top talent and keep them happy, engaged, and, critically, *at the office*. The workplace became a tool for building a brand and a community.

The Hybrid Office and the Age of Choice

Then came the COVID-19 pandemic. It forced the world into the biggest remote-work experiment in history and, in doing so, accelerated trends that were already bubbling under the surface. It shattered the long-held belief that serious work could only happen when everyone was in the same building from 9 to 5.

We've now entered the era of the hybrid office. Today's information worker is more autonomous than ever and expects the flexibility to choose where and when they do their best work. This has forced companies, employees, and designers alike to address a fundamental question: what is an office even *for*?

The answer is no longer simply "a place for individual work." For many, that's what home is for. Instead, the office now functions like a "clubhouse," a destination for the things we can't do over Zoom. Currently, the workplace fills the following roles, and the design has followed suit:

Social hub
> A place designed for collaboration, team-building, and brainstorming. Think fewer individual desks and more flexible, high-tech meeting rooms and casual gathering spaces.

Cultural anchor
> A place to connect with colleagues, mentor new hires, and absorb company culture, things that are harder to do in a virtual space.

Flexible resource
> A place to meet up in person, if needed. Smart technology now allows employees to book a desk or a meeting room with an app, making the office a seamless, on-demand resource to take advantage of rather than a daily requirement to commute to.

The story of the office, when viewed through the lens of history, has evolved from a place of control to a place of empowerment. The design of our workplaces will continue to change, but it will always be a mirror of our culture and history at large, reflecting the tools, management styles, and, most importantly, the ever-changing nature of how we think, create, and work together.

The Future Is Listening

More than ever, in a world of infinite choice, we need Design Democracy to make decisions that work for everyone. We're all in flux in this new landscape of hybrid work.

The history of work trends and their resulting workplace designs has immense value in teaching us what *not* to do and how to avoid the distortion of good ideas. Modern corporate culture still has a tendency to pound every new idea into an old template, blowing right past the critically important patterns at the heart of an organization's true essence. The future of work and workplace design, if we're to learn from our past, is about listening, finding those patterns, and holding on to them in ways that allow design to elevate culture.

I'm optimistic about what artificial intelligence holds for architecture and real estate development. When we create private visual and narrative surveys and other interactive spaces where people feel safe telling us the truth about what they want, in their own way, then we will have the right prompts to feed into the engine of artificial intelligence. But we must ask the right questions if we want to get the right answers. As of today, if you ask an AI to design a 10,000-square-foot space for a creative technology firm, it will spit out a perfectly good design from ten years ago. It wouldn't be wrong, necessarily, but it will be an average of our past, not a vision for the future.

The future of getting projects right, whether as an architect or a real estate developer, will entail mastering the art of asking the right questions—of our users and of ourselves. So, with this in mind, where do we begin designing for our modern, hybrid work? What elements should we consider? Where is the heartbeat of the current, twenty-first-century company, and how can we ensure its pulse is felt throughout the spaces we create? And what are the right questions? You've probably already been asking them, but not to the right people, not to the group. That's the key—you probably have great inspiration pictures, and great questions to determine workstyle and how products are produced, but if these questions are only being asked at the top, it won't matter how good the artificial intelligence is; it won't be thinking about the right people.

The Kitchen Is the Heart

Sharing a meal is a fundamental human activity that builds community. People want to sit and eat while talking to other people. In the modern workplace, sharing a meal holds immense value. It fosters in-person connection in an increasingly digital world, breaking down hierarchies and creating opportunities for impromptu collaboration. This simultaneously intimate and informal interaction has become paramount as offices have evolved from "information factories" to "knowledge hubs."

A lunch table is a level playing field. It removes the formal structure of a meeting, and the result is a more casual connection between colleagues. Sharing stories about life outside of work builds the trust and empathy that form the bedrock of effective teamwork. In a hybrid world, these moments are more critical than ever. When an engineer, a marketer, and a designer sit together to share a meal, they share perspectives more readily than in the stiff, removed setting of a boardroom. This typically sparks conversations that lead to innovation.

Additionally, when everyone from the CEO to the intern eats in the same café, it sends a powerful message of a democratic culture and opens the flow of communication. In this flattened, less hierarchical setting, leadership is far more approachable.

Think back to the Taylorist offices, where the break area was a windowless afterthought. Later, the staff cafeteria was designed for speed, not connection. It was tech companies like Google and Pixar that understood that a well-designed canteen could be a core part of their innovation strategy. Maybe your version of this critical space is different. A café can be designed for "creative friction," placed at a central crossroads to encourage mingling. Or it can be designed to inspire, situated in a spot that perfectly captures an expansive view of the sunset, and where people leave refreshed, ready to offer their best work.

Just as the kitchen has become the social center of the modern home, it has also become the heart of the modern office. It's now a destination, a place people *want* to be. Today, this "kitchen" is arguably one of the most important zones in the hybrid office, and it's not solely about food anymore. It's a multi-purpose space for informal meetings, solo work, and, most importantly, the central point for rebuilding the social fabric of a distributed team.

The Search for What Is Real

The architect's greatest tool is observation. You have to survey people, yes, but you also have to watch them in action, because sometimes people can't accurately tell you why or how they do something. Spend a few days in their environment before doing any surveys. Act like an anthropologist and observe.

You're searching for the unwritten rules of an organization, their hidden workflows, and the real human needs lurking beneath the surface of their job titles. Keep these critical questions in mind as you observe:

- How, when, and where do people truly connect and collaborate?
- What technologies are essential arteries of communication, and where is technology an unwanted intrusion?
- Who truly needs dedicated, private space, and who thrives in the open?
- How does the flow of light, traffic, and energy throughout the day change the way the space feels and functions?

Keep the basics in mind, too. Design for the easily detectable mess. Dealing with trash, stacks of paper, coffee mugs, jackets piled over desk chairs, etc., shouldn't be part of the daily rhythm of a workplace. Make trash and recycling easy. If the company is going paperless, make scanning intuitive. In a cold climate, give people a place for their coats. Make sure the basics are covered, even as you keep an eye out for their bigger needs.

Pay particular attention to the presence and/or absence of the three key patterns of Design Democracy, each of which addresses our fundamental human needs: physical comfort, human interaction, and self-care. Every great workplace, regardless of budget or style, is built upon these patterns.

The Ultimate Test

After this in-person study, it's time to craft the right questions for your surveys—the true work of Design Democracy. You are not just collecting data with these surveys; you are holding up a mirror to an organization, asking the people you've studied to reflect on the culture you've observed. Look for the patterns in their answers. If your data sets are large enough, use artificial intelligence to find the signal in the noise. You won't get everyone to participate, but between forty-five to fifty-five percent of them will, and that is orders of magnitude more listening than anyone else is doing.

Remember that the Design Democracy process is about more than just designing a better office. It's an act of engagement. People want to be asked, and they want to be heard.

Which brings us to the ultimate test of all this work. Companies now making policies that *require* their employees to return to the office are trying to force something to happen that we all want to occur more naturally. For some companies, it's essential to get back in the office. The workplace should naturally align with the essential need to be there.

The goal of a successful workplace design is not to build a beautiful cage. The goal is to create a place with its own gravity. A place that helps people do their best work, forge meaningful connections, and feel valued as human beings. If the office is done right, it will be used. People *want* to go to a place that enables them to do things they can't do anywhere else. That is the only return-to-office mandate that will ever work.

Chapter 9:

Dream Teams

I love David Goggins and Laird Hamilton. I've read their books, and they've undoubtedly pushed me to do more push-ups, run harder, and lift more. But the true gift these men offer is far greater than a jolt of motivation; it's a framework for facing the constant practice of struggle and a profound understanding of its value. Their philosophies, born from the fire of extreme physical and mental challenges, provide a powerful antidote to the pervasive issue of privilege that plagues so many industries, especially design and real estate.

David Goggins famously said, "We don't rise to the level of our expectations, we fall to the level of our training." This is a stark and vital truth. We can all aspire to excellence, but when the pressure mounts, when the stakes are real, it's not some idealized version of ourselves, our abilities, or our work that will carry us through. It's the core strength we've forged through relentless, repetitive practice that saves the day. The underlying idea of Goggins' words is that we have to practice perfection so that our baseline performance is above average. True perfection might only grace us occasionally, but establishing a foundation of rigorous training ensures that, even on our worst days, we are still competent, reliable, and capable of delivering.

This concept of falling to the level of our training is not just about physical feats; it's a metaphor for professional and personal development, too. In the world of design and real estate, where projects are complex, budgets are tight, and emotions run high, our "training" is cultivating empathy, shedding our privileges, and relentlessly pursuing a deeper understanding of the human experience in all its messy reality.

The Character of Empathy

When we intentionally seek out challenges that don't benefit from our inherent privileges, we stretch our capacity for empathy and compassion. Difficult paths often have the best views. Exposing yourself to something that is intimidating but not truly dangerous is a powerful way to build character.

But what is "character" in the context of professional excellence? It is the antithesis of a privileged mindset. Having character means not acting entitled—as if you're someone who deserves certain gifts or should be shielded from difficult situations simply because of who you are. It is a practiced way of being if you're born with or acquire a wealth of privileges. But when you develop this character, you develop empathy, allowing you to understand what a design actually needs to serve everyone.

Empathy should be the spark that ignites the design process. It's the critical moments of insight—the profound understanding of what another person truly needs. But insight alone is powerless. To turn that spark into a meaningful solution, it requires something to push it. Character is the cultivated strength to embrace adversity, to remain steadfast when a challenge tempts you to compromise, and to consistently choose the harder right over the easier wrong. It's the internal fortitude that transforms good intentions into deliberate action.

That action, the tangible expression of empathy and character, is compassion. Compassion is the ultimate act of design. It's not just feeling for someone but actively doing something for them. This means courageously stepping outside your comfort zone to seek out the perspectives you don't hold and the experiences you haven't lived. It involves facing difficult truths, listening to inconvenient feedback, and designing for humanity in all its messy, unpredictable reality. When you lead with this compassionate framework, you build more than just a product or a space; you foster stronger relationships, drive more inclusive decisions, and cultivate a resilience that can weather any storm. This approach earns genuine respect, not from a title or unearned status, but from a demonstrated commitment to your shared humanity.

Laird Hamilton has a quote that perfectly illustrates the resiliency that comes from shedding privilege and facing difficulty head-on: "All the people I know who have been bitten by sharks are less afraid of sharks now." That, of course, is exposure therapy in its most extreme form. But the truth behind it is the same: by confronting a fear, by surviving it, the fear loses its power. The imagined horror of something is almost always worse than its reality.

This is a crucial lesson for those of us in positions of influence. We must be willing to "get bitten" by the realities of our clients' and end-users' experiences. We must be willing to step outside of our comfortable bubbles and confront the anxieties, frustrations, and fears of those who are not steeped in the jargon and complexities of design. These anxieties, frustrations, and fears are an unavoidable part of the design and construction process, whether we face them head-on or not.

To make good on developing my own character, I took up martial arts—initially on a dare from my wife—and quickly fell in love with its raw authenticity. The first time you get punched in the gut, your privilege evaporates. In the dojo, no one cares where you came from, what school you attended, or how much money you make. It was, and still is, a great equalizer. The more I let go of that armor of privilege, the more I empathized with those who never had it in the first place. And the more I empathized with people and groups in general, the better designer I became.

The Privilege Problem in Design and Real Estate

Addressing privilege and actively working to dismantle it is crucial as a designer because the real estate and design industries have a deeply ingrained privilege problem, and for a long time, I was a part of it.

My first wake-up call to my own privilege came on a construction site. I was twelve years old, and my parents, with their New England school-of-hard-knocks mentality, figured some manual labor would do me good. Perhaps because my family was full of bankers and insurance providers, their interpretation of feeding my architectural calling was to burnish me in the crucible of a real jobsite. Whether it was intentional or accidental, it worked. The yearly summer ritual of carpentry, light electrical work, and moving endless piles of lumber always eased the edges off my sense of entitlement.

I remember my first day, absolutely convinced that the seasoned carpenters and tradesmen would rush to hear my brilliant design ideas. In my mind, my passion for architecture gave me a seat at the table. Instead, I was handed a broom. I was asked to do the only thing I was qualified for: sweep floors, shovel sawdust, and make sure the dumpster was efficiently packed. In the years that followed, I graduated to lead carpenter's assistant, layout, cutting, and nailing all day. Still, no one asked for my design input, and they certainly weren't interested when I volunteered it. This was my first lesson in the difference between passion and qualification.

It took a while, but eventually, I asked the right questions. It was the fall of 1998, my first job in California, and the last time I worked in the field. Instead of broadcasting my design abilities, I started asking the crew what *they* thought was deficient in the plans they had to build from. Were these problems consistent from project to project? How would *they* reinvent the process? The response was a revelation. Suddenly, everyone wanted to engage. Suggestions came from all sides. These were my first, raw insights into the power of listening—my first intuitive attempt at Design Democracy. And a funny thing happened: the more I listened to them, the more they started to listen to me. This was my first experience with the two-way empathy portal that mutual respect creates. A few months later, I was put in a project management role, but I never forgot that first lesson in the power of seeking out the "missing voices."

So many designers come from a place of privilege, either because their families could afford to support their passion for the arts over more practical career paths, or because they developed a "privileged soul" as a result of the mystical, often revered, position that design holds in the project cycle. There's nothing inherently wrong with either of these paths, but they require a strong dose of temperance. If this is your starting point, you'll need to undergo a conscious conversion from privilege to empathy in order to create truly effective and collaborative teams.

This privilege is not just a social issue; it's putting the very practice of architecture in danger. The profession has drifted away from the nitty-gritty of needs analysis, due diligence, and project management, often in favor of a more esoteric, artistic pursuit. Within that pursuit lies the dangerous and misleading tendency to chase trends over solving and designing for the enduring patterns of human behavior and need.

The path forward entails both a widespread recognition of the privilege within the design profession and an individual pursuit of empathy-based character within each of our careers. Only then can we embrace design as a truly democratic process.

But how do we get there? One of the most critical acts of empathy is understanding the stress, disruption, and fear that many people experience during the design and project process. For someone outside the industry, it's a terrifying, expensive, and entirely new world fraught with hundreds of decisions that take place in a completely foreign language. Questions abound for someone just starting into the process: How do I select engineers? How do I choose a general contractor? How do I protect myself from being taken advantage of? Who do I buy furniture from, and who will help me select it? How do I even begin planning to move 654 people from one side of town to the other?

My team and I may have the answers to most of these questions, but simply stating that up front is not the solution. People don't want to be told what to do; they want their fears and concerns to be heard. They want their teams to be heard and their problems seen. They need what I call "Enterprise-Level Empathy": a deep, organizational commitment to understanding and addressing the human element at every stage of the project.

This is where the lessons of organizational psychology come into play. Overconfidence in leaders and consultants is a major obstacle to achieving Enterprise-Level Empathy. Overconfidence from those leaders and consultants is a key part of this problem, as it signals a fundamental lack of self-awareness and an unwillingness to learn from those within their organization. This inevitably leads to poor decision-making and a toxic project environment.

Overconfident designers and brokers also create an environment of low psychological safety. They can be dismissive of feedback, intolerant of mistakes, and loath to admit their own errors. This stifles innovation and discourages team members and clients from speaking up during the process or learning from it. When people don't feel safe to be vulnerable, creativity withers, and a culture of hiding problems takes root. And no one can solve problems that stay hidden.

This overconfidence also breeds groupthink. When a leader is overly sure of their own abilities, they are less likely to seek out diverse perspectives or conduct thorough due diligence. Team members, sensing this, may conform to the leader's opinion to avoid conflict, often leading to flawed strategies and disastrous outcomes. This erodes the very foundation of effective leadership, and Design Democracy dies or is never engaged in the first place with these kinds of leaders.

It's all too common for clients, brokers, and architects to come across as arrogant and unapproachable, making it difficult for them to connect with their teams on a human level. Their lack of humility and relatability signals a closed-off attitude to learning and development, which can alienate team members and lead to a further decline in morale and engagement. Leaders who believe they have all the answers don't typically seek out new information or adapt their strategies, creating a stagnant and uninspired organizational culture. All of this deeply affects the design process.

Don't work with these clients. It's not worth it, and you won't reach a truly successful end result because the foundation is flawed from the start. The risk of these projects outweighs the reward. And don't hire these kinds of brokers either, or you will be in danger of not getting the best thing for your company; worse, you'll likely get a rushed process that results in too much space and a higher lifetime bill than you bargained for. Most importantly, don't hire a designer of any kind who is not completely focused on listening and establishing Enterprise-Level Empathy from the start of a project to a finished space.

Designing for Real Life: The Curb Cut Effect and Stress Cases

To truly embrace Enterprise-Level Empathy, we must fundamentally shift our design philosophy. We need to convert our teams into groups that are deeply invested in understanding the intricate and intersecting points of the triangle of making a space: people, patterns, and reality. This means actively seeking out the "stress cases" of a project, often found within the "edge case" user groups whose problems are often overlooked.

In their book *Design for Real Life*, Eric Meyer and Sara Wachter-Boettcher introduce a powerful concept: designing for "stress cases" rather than dismissing them as mere "edge cases." An edge case is a rare problem affecting a small minority, making it easy to ignore. Viewing these problems as stress cases, however, reframes the issue these groups are dealing with—we're no longer simply dealing with the problem of a fringe user, we're helping users who are facing a fringe situation. These users could be anyone in a moment of crisis, distraction, or distress, and this shift in perspective is an act of empathy that leads to a more compassionate and effective design overall.

By focusing on these stress cases, like the person trying to close a deceased relative's account, the user navigating a complex interface after a car accident, or someone simply having a terrible day, we are forced to design with a deeper level of compassion. This approach challenges us to build systems that are clear, forgiving, and supportive when users have the least amount of cognitive energy to spare.

The core argument for this approach to design is that compassion has universal benefits. When a design works well for someone at their most vulnerable, it works exponentially better for everyone else in their everyday lives. A process that is simple enough for a user in crisis is effortlessly clear for a user at their best. Just as curb cuts, designed for wheelchair users, benefit parents with strollers and travelers with luggage, designing for stress cases creates a more resilient, humane, and accessible experience for all. It's not just about being nice; it's about recognizing the messy reality of human life and building things that don't break when people are already broken. It's a proactive form of empathy-based character embedded into the very fabric of a product or service.

Keep this principle at the core of every design project. Who are the "stress cases" in your project? What kind of "curb cut" can you create? Are you helping the new employee who is navigating the office for the first time? The neurodivergent individual who is sensitive to noise and light? The person with a temporary mobility issue? By focusing on their needs, by designing with their challenges in mind, we can create spaces that are not just beautiful, but also intuitive, comfortable, and truly inclusive.

A Core Design Guide for Anyone

The design process itself can be a major source of stress and anxiety for clients. Demystifying this process is a crucial step in building trust and fostering a collaborative environment. While there is no single, one-size-fits-all process, there are several key elements, milestones, and best practices that can help guide the journey: prioritizing collaboration, ensuring project flow, hiring the right experts, having budget conversations, and knowing when to bring certain people and stakeholders into the design process. Let's go over each of these in more detail.

Prioritizing Collaboration

Meet weekly with the project team, including the client, no matter what. Even if it's only for 15 minutes. When people ask me why I am able to get projects done in such short timelines, it's because I prioritize weekly meetings. When asked how we're able to keep complicated projects on budget, it's because I prioritize weekly meetings. I could go on like this, but you get my point. If you have to answer for something every week, nothing gets too far off base. A pro tip on this is scheduling these meetings on a Tuesday, Wednesday, or Thursday. No one is prepared for meetings on Monday, and everyone forgets what they committed to on Friday.

Ensuring Project Flow

The design and project process typically breaks down into the following phases: pre-design (or programming), schematic design, design development, construction documents, bidding and negotiation, and construction administration. It's essential for the design team to clearly explain what each of these phases entails, what decisions need to be made and when, and how to phase the expected timeline. This should be a transparent and iterative process. Make sure all the approving people are available when they need to be. Be decisive, follow the data, and don't be afraid to make small changes later. Hold a ten to fifteen percent contingency and plan to spend it. There will be things you want to do later that you can't foresee in the beginning.

Hiring the Right Experts

The selection process for hiring experts is critical. Get emotional here. Don't worry too much about the price of the designers, as it's a fraction of the project cost and has a huge impact on everything that follows. Make sure you can work with these people. Make sure they listen and have a process for listening to your people. You're not necessarily looking for the most talented designer; you're looking for the *right* designer for your project and your team. Avoid designers who speak solely in jargon and parrot trend after trend about your industry. Your vision needs to emerge. Their vision should be secondary. Look for designers who are curious, committed to understanding your needs and goals, and willing to demystify the design language.

Having Budget Conversations

Budget is often a source of great discomfort for clients, and the costs abound. Renting office space is expensive. Constructing office space is expensive. Both have a range of costs and elicit a variety of questions. How much should I spend? Should I tell my team how much I have to spend? Should I tell them half that number? Who can I trust? All of these are good questions. And I've seen the budget handled in nearly every way possible.

The truth is that something can be built, with certain caveats, for whatever you are comfortable spending. But the most important part of the budget is this: Be clear about what you want to spend. Don't hide the ball. If the team gets the impression that you are not being clear, then they will start to guess, and the price will go up. They might get the impression that there is no limit to what they can spend. Any later conversation about conserving cost won't have any real validity because they know you've withheld the real number from them, and they can't necessarily trust your word. If you set an artificial limit but then make changes like there is no limit, others will notice.

Be real about the numbers and how you got to that estimate. Tell your design candidates what you want to accomplish and ask for their thoughts on an estimate; what do they think it should cost? Encourage them to support their responses with evidence from the general contractors they work with. Chances are, they'll have similar answers, so talk to the outliers. They might have good reasons for giving you a number that stands out from the rest, but get rid of those suggestions if they're not backed up with solid reasoning and experience. Ask questions about how the design firms and construction companies are using artificial intelligence. In 2026, if your design team is not using artificial intelligence to improve your plans, round out your estimate, and tighten your code compliance, then you are losing out. That design team is behind the times, and likely charging too much as a result.

Any good design team will approach these budget conversations with transparency and empathy. They will help you understand where your money is going, where it makes sense to invest, and where you can potentially cut costs without compromising your core goals. These budget conversations should always be tied to your project goals; because the goals of each project vary, the right budget strategy is different for everyone.

Knowing When to Bring People In

The question of when to bring in various stakeholders is a crucial one, but the answer is rather simple: as early as possible. The more people who are involved in the early stages of the design process, the more likely you are to create a space that truly meets the needs of its users. This includes bringing in not just the C-suite but representatives from different departments, facilities staff, and a diverse group of end users as well.

By embracing the principles of Design Democracy, by shedding our privileges and cultivating a deep sense of empathy, we can transform the design and real estate industries. We can move from an opaque, intimidating, and often exclusionary process to one that is transparent, collaborative, and truly human-centered. We can create spaces that not only function well and look beautiful but that also foster a sense of belonging, well-being, and shared purpose.

This is the promise of Enterprise-Level Empathy, and it is a future worth fighting for.

Chapter 10:

Consensus, Compromise, and Truth

Remember the nearly averted disaster of the rushed brokerage transaction from Chapter 5? The large organization careening toward workplace hell at the hands of a team with a dangerously narrow set of priorities? Well, it's time I told you how we turned that project around.

Just as this multi-million-dollar real estate deal was about to be vaporized, everyone turned to us. We'd been sidelined for months, offering strategic design guidance only to be politely but firmly shut out. "The landlord's in-house space planner has it all under control," they continually assured us. Then, suddenly, their neat formulas, their industry averages, and their one-size-fits-all assumptions stopped providing the right answers. With only weeks before they needed to ink the deal, the confidence that had buoyed the project for months evaporated, replaced by a cold, creeping panic.

What happened next isn't just a cautionary tale about real estate; it's the perfect case study to dismantle the myth of the focus group and prove the transformative power of Design Democracy. Before our involvement, the project's original architect had interviewed the entire leadership team. They conducted focus groups, workshops, and roundtables—the classic tools of corporate due diligence. The problem was, the information they gathered was nearly useless. In these public sessions, people said profoundly different things from what they expressed in private. To put it bluntly, they lied. Not maliciously, but defensively. They publicly voiced what they thought everyone else wanted to hear and, most critically, what they assumed their boss wanted to hear. The room was thick with the silent, suffocating pressure of conformity. Timur Kuran's concept of "preference falsification"—the tendency of well-intentioned people in professional settings to systematically misrepresent their own needs and desires—was on full, painful display.

In his book, *Private Truths, Public Lies*, economist Timur Kuran provides a powerful framework for understanding this phenomenon. He argues that we all face the constant negotiation between our genuine, private preferences and the preferences we end up expressing to others. What we voice in public is influenced by the perceived social and personal consequences of revealing our true thoughts.

In our client's focus groups, for example, the calculus of each participant was simple and subconscious. Expressing a private truth, like "I desperately need a quiet place to concentrate," or "Our team never uses these large boardrooms; we need smaller huddle spaces," carried a risk. Would this personal, private need, voiced out loud, make them seem difficult? Would it contradict the opinion of a powerful senior vice president? Would they be labeled "not a team player" for complaining about the proposed plan? The potential cost of honesty felt high, while the benefit of speaking their truth and expressing their real needs in the workplace seemed abstract and uncertain. Would it make a difference to say their real opinions about the proposed plan, or would that just hurt them in the long run?

Conversely, expressing a public lie, or, more accurately, a sanitized and agreeable version of the truth, was the path of least resistance for those in the focus group. Nodding along with the consensus, endorsing the boss's vague platitudes about "synergy" and "collaboration," and accepting the landlord's generic floor plan felt safer. It minimized friction and maintained social harmony. The tragic irony is that when everyone in the room makes this same rational, self-preserving calculation, the collective outcome is a decision that serves no one. The public consensus becomes a fiction that everyone privately despises but publicly upholds. This is precisely where our client was heading: toward a beautiful, expensive, and utterly dysfunctional new headquarters built upon a foundation of well-mannered lies.

The transaction team, blind to this dynamic, took the focus group's feedback at face value. They checked the box on "employee engagement" and proceeded with a plan that reflected the fictional consensus. But they were now operating on a ghost signal, a distorted echo of what people actually needed. My team and I knew there was a better way. We knew, with absolute certainty, that there was plenty of space to create a workplace people would actually love, not just say they loved to save face. And we knew this not because of a gut feeling or a clever design trick but because of the data we gathered. Unfalsified, unvarnished, privately sourced data.

In the years preceding this critical moment, my team and I had done the very work that the transaction team feared and dismissed as unnecessary. We had engaged in the democratic discovery process of Design Democracy, which purposefully and thoroughly sidestepped the pitfalls of public performance. We had already put our structured, data-centric methodology for gathering, analyzing, and acting upon employee input to use. We had already created workplaces that reflected a company's unique cultural DNA. We knew our process would work again. Designing a successful workplace is a cultural exercise first, a design exercise second, and that's how we approached this project, too.

We began again in earnest—now no longer sidelined—by measuring reality. We analyzed how our client *actually* used their old space, tracking utilization rates with sensors and observational studies. We mapped movement patterns to understand which pathways got clogged and which remained unused. We didn't just count heads; we understood the rhythm of their work—how frequently people were physically in the office, where they naturally congregated once there, and where they consistently struggled to find the right kind of space to do their work. This quantitative data gave us a picture of the organization's actual behavior, stripped of opinion and politics.

More importantly, we asked real questions of real people in ways that felt safer than traditional focus groups. We privately surveyed hundreds of people across the organization, from the most senior executives to the newest junior hires. The platform we used was confidential, creating a space for honest feedback and allowing for the kind of candor that's impossible to reach in a conference room with someone's boss sitting at the head of the table. In our private online surveys, we asked about their work: their daily tasks, their biggest frustrations with the current environment, and their aspirations for a better way of working. We asked about their cultural experiences: What did they value? What did they want more of?

It turned out that what the workforce at this company really wanted was neither frivolous nor outrageous. Their desires were deeply practical and surprisingly consistent. They wanted more conference rooms, but of varied sizes, especially small, two-to-four-person rooms for impromptu conversations. They craved more informal, comfortable places to connect with colleagues outside of a formal meeting structure. They wanted better amenities for lunch and coffee, not as a perk but as a utility that would save them time and foster community. And they expressed an overwhelming desire for greater access to natural light and the outdoors. These were not the pie-in-the-sky demands of a spoiled workforce, as the brokerage team imagined; they were the fundamental requirements for a productive and humane modern workplace.

Our Design Democracy process yielded thousands of data points, but one crucial finding eclipsed all others: Due to the nature of their work—a mix of in-office collaboration, focused individual work, remote flexibility, and client site visits—there would never be more than sixty-two percent of the organization in the office at any given time. This single metric, our "peak utilization rate," changed everything. It was the key that unlocked the entire puzzle. It meant the company didn't need a dedicated seat for every single one of their employees. Building a one-to-one desk ratio, the unquestioned assumption of the landlord's plan, would have been a colossal waste of money, space, and opportunity. The better plan involved shared space and resources—as most modern organizations will find moving forward. At this company, we designed space for a small number of employees with specific roles. But for the vast majority of employees, a flexible, shared environment would not only suffice for their office needs but would actively enhance their work experience by freeing up space for all the other elements they told us they desperately needed.

Building Trust: Reciprocity in Action

The Design Democracy process of creating a safe channel for individuals to share their private truths does more than just yield better data. It fundamentally alters the relationship between employees and leadership. It's a real-world application of the core concept from Robert Axelrod's groundbreaking book, *The Evolution of Cooperation*. Axelrod studied game theory and found that the most successful strategy for fostering long-term cooperation was simple: cooperate on the first move, and thereafter, do whatever your opponent did on their previous move. It's a strategy of initial optimism, followed by direct reciprocity. Axelrod called this strategy "Tit for Tat."

In the corporate world, change initiatives often elicit cynicism and distrust because employees have been "betrayed" by these initiatives in the past. Leaders announce their commitment to a new era of listening, but their actions don't match their words. The Design Democracy process, particularly sending out a confidential, comprehensive survey to every employee, is a way for leadership to send a powerful message: "We trust you to tell us the truth. We value your honest input, and we are creating a safe mechanism for you to provide it."

This isn't just another empty announcement or another memo from HR; it's a tangible demonstration of trust. When employees see this, they are far more likely to reciprocate. They respond with candid, thoughtful feedback because the risk of being honest has been removed. This initiates a virtuous cycle. Leadership receives valuable, truthful data. They use that data to make visibly better decisions. Employees see the results of their participation. We present the findings to leadership and the broader group so they can understand how their feedback translated into real-world improvements, like the addition of smaller meeting rooms in the new design or better coffee options in the café, which then validates their decision to be honest. This, in turn, makes them even more willing to offer cooperative feedback in the future.

Trust is built through this reciprocal loop of action and response. The simple act of asking employees for their feedback, then acting on their answers, transforms the dynamic of the design process from a top-down mandate into a collaborative partnership.

From Fear to Feedback: The Gentle Exposure Therapy of Design Democracy

If this process is so powerful, why doesn't every organization do it? Because the leadership's fear of losing control is too strong. Will asking for their employees' opinions be considered a sign of weakness? Will it open a Pandora's box of criticism they can't handle? These questions aren't easy, and corporations often fear the messiness of human emotion and the unpredictability of collective desire. Essentially, they fear knowing the truth.

But good things often come from being uncomfortable, and the beauty of the Design Democracy framework is that it provides a structured way to move through this discomfort. It begins with the safest, lowest-risk step: the private, individual survey. This allows people to express their true opinions without fear of social judgment. It acts as a gentle form of exposure therapy for an organization allergic to honest feedback. These surveys convey what their workforce actually thinks in a low-stakes, approachable way.

The next step is synthesizing and presenting this data back to the group in an aggregated, anonymous form. Instead of saying, "John in accounting thinks the open plan is too loud," we can say, "Sixty-eight percent of respondents expressed a need for more access to quiet, focused workplaces." This depersonalizes the feedback. It's no longer one person's complaint; it's a quantifiable, collective reality: its Evidence-Based Empathy in action. This step is a vital part of the Design Democracy process, as it exposes people to the *true* consensus within an organization, often dramatically different from the *public* consensus. It breaks the spell of groupthink by showing individuals that their private truths are, in fact, often widely shared. This gives them the confidence and the social proof to begin aligning their public statements with their private beliefs.

The challenge of this step is not gathering the input; employees are more than willing to share their opinion when given a safe invitation to do so. The challenge is leadership's willingness to confront their own fears and truly listen to their workforce.

The Art of Synthesis: From Crowdsourcing to Coherent Design

Data makes everything easier. It turns subjective arguments into objective conversations. Instead of leaders imposing their personal preferences for an open-plan office onto their workforce, they can point to data showing that seventy percent of employees want a hybrid model with a mix of open and enclosed spaces. Data provides political cover for making bold, necessary changes like these because it depersonalizes decisions, basing them on data-driven solutions instead of personal preference.

Design Democracy doesn't abdicate professional responsibility; it arms creative experts with better information. It doesn't outsource design; it crowdsources insight.

The design team's role in this process is not to be passive poll-takers. We are data analysts, cultural anthropologists, and strategic designers. Our job is to synthesize diverse input into a set of viable, coherent options. Technology makes this process efficient and scalable. The Design Democracy platform allows teams to pose questions, gather both quantitative and qualitative feedback, and analyze the results in real time. For example, the design team can ask employees for their private vote on various design concepts and what amenities to prioritize, or to share their thoughts on everything from lighting to acoustics. The platform then visualizes this data, making it easier for the team to identify clear trends, points of consensus, and areas of contention.

The art and science of design come into play with this synthesis. In the instance of that rushed brokerage deal that our design team was tasked to save, our expert synthesis saved the day in an otherwise impossible situation. More meeting rooms, *and* informal lounge space, *and* better amenities wouldn't have fit within the given square footage had we not uncovered the crucial sixty-two percent peak utilization data point. That data point revealed the solution: by eliminating the assumed necessity of the one-desk-per-person approach, we could unlock vast amounts of space to work in the variety of collaborative, focused, and social spaces that employees craved.

Armed with this mountain of data, we walked back into the negotiation with the landlord and the transaction team. The atmosphere had changed completely. We weren't presenting a subjective design opinion; we were presenting an unassailable case for a design built on the expressed needs and observed behaviors of their own people. The landlord's space plans were not just inadequate; they were fundamentally, demonstrably wrong. They were based on outdated assumptions about how people work. Our plans, in contrast, were a direct reflection of the organization's unique cultural DNA.

The data became both a shield and a sword in moving forward with the project. It shielded the client's financial and cultural interests from the landlord's low-cost, low-value proposal. And it cut through the fog of assumptions and generic "best practices" that had previously paralyzed the process. We could point to the numbers that proved our proposed design would not only fit comfortably within the building's footprint but would also dramatically improve the employee experience and the company's operational effectiveness.

Things that might have felt like bold, risky choices, such as reducing the number of dedicated desks by nearly forty percent, no longer felt like a gamble. We could show that hundreds of people were in favor of a more flexible model if it meant getting more collaborative and amenity spaces in return. The fear of getting their employees' input, which had haunted the leadership team, was replaced by the confidence of data-driven clarity.

In the case of our client, the final results were staggering. By embracing this democratic, data-driven approach, we designed a more effective and efficient space. We demonstrated to the landlord that their initial assessment was incorrect, and they conceded to a design that truly met the client's needs as a result—all while fitting into a smaller overall footprint. We doubled their number of client-facing meeting spaces, directly enhancing the company's business development capabilities. And, the number that resonated most powerfully in the C-suite, we reduced their overall rent expenditure by forty-five percent, simply by eliminating the wasted space of unused, unwanted desks. The final outcome was a workplace where everyone felt heard, which dramatically increased company engagement and morale long before the first moving truck arrived.

The transaction team's greatest fear—that involving the design team and the employees early on would complicate and jeopardize the deal—was unfounded. In fact, the opposite was true. Our early involvement, grounded in the principles of Design Democracy, would've saved the deal from being at risk of imploding in the first place, and it's what clarified a solution in the end. We didn't just fix the landlord's flawed plan; we created a strategic asset for the company—a powerful tool to attract and retain talent, and a physical manifestation of their unique and newly trusting culture. We turned a real estate transaction into a cultural transformation. Collective intelligence replaced fearing the truth. And in that shift, we found not chaos but a better, more human, and more profitable way to build the future of work.

What this story ultimately demonstrates is that the hardest part of transformation isn't drafting floor plans, negotiating leases, or selecting furniture. It's creating the right conditions for truth to emerge. It's having the courage, at every level of an organization, to confront people's real needs, not just what they say in public or what tradition dictates. Design Democracy prioritizes honesty over appearances, curiosity over certainty, and collaboration over hierarchy.

When organizations embrace Design Democracy, the payoff is profound; they unlock the full potential of their people, their culture, and their spaces. The lesson of this approach is simple but powerful: The truth, when gathered thoughtfully, acted upon decisively, and shared transparently, is the ultimate design tool. Consensus, compromise, and courage turn knowledge into action, conflict into creativity, and vision into reality. And as our experience shows, when you give people the space to be honest, you can create workplaces and organizations that thrive far beyond expectations.

Chapter 11:

Courage to Innovate

Innovation isn't an abstract business strategy; it's a deeply human act of courage. It begins not in a boardroom with spreadsheets, but in the internal decision to push off into the unknown, to trade the comfort of the proven for the potential of the extraordinary. It's a feeling of profound vulnerability balanced on the edge of possibility. We've all felt this before, long before we had careers or deadlines. We felt it the moment our parents let go of the bicycle seat and we were self-propelled for the first time on two wheels, wobbling and uncertain, propelled forward by nothing more than trust in ourselves.

That single moment, the one that contains fear, balance, momentum, and the promise of a new kind of freedom, is the courage to innovate. The story of a bike ride is the story of every team that ever dared to launch a new idea. It contains all the essential lessons on navigating ambiguity, recovering from a fall, and finding the grit to pedal up the steepest of hills. As we go deeper into the mechanics of innovation, we must connect with the simple, foundational courage it requires.

In the summer of 1998, a few months after graduating from Cornell, I rode my bicycle across the United States. It wasn't a plan; it was a departure. A departure from the meticulously paved career paths my friends were taking, and a departure from the comfortable, predictable world I had always known.

It was the first truly difficult thing I had ever chosen to do—an endurance test designed to strip away the noise of expectation and see what was left. That bike ride was my answer to the quiet, nagging feeling that the life prescribed to me wasn't my own. By the time I staggered onto a California beach ten weeks later, I felt like I'd lived my entire life up to that point in slow motion. That journey, confronting fear, dismantling my ego, pushing through brutal monotony and unexpected failure, was a foundational education. I can trace every significant lesson I've learned about innovation, persistence, and creativity back to specific moments on that long, lonely road. It's where I learned that to build anything new, you have to first answer the right call, then be willing to humble yourself to the unknown.

Answering the Right Call

In *The Hero with a Thousand Faces*, Joseph Campbell describes the first stage of the archetypal journey as the "call to adventure," a moment that signifies that "a destiny has summoned the hero and transferred his spiritual center of gravity from within the pale of his society to a zone unknown." Internal conflict within the hero is the essence of Campbell's call to adventure: the familiar world is no longer enough, but the path forward remains terrifyingly unclear.

That bike ride was never part of a plan. The plan, as far as I knew, was to land some great, spirit-aligned, yet-to-be-defined, super career right out of college. For my fellow seniors and highly motivated friends, the answer to "What's next?" was already settled: working prestigious jobs at financial services firms or studying for med school entrance exams. But their certainty felt foreign to me, like a superhighway I had no desire to merge onto. I had a different question echoing in my mind: Did I want a job, or did I want to move to Fiji and teach windsurfing? I honestly didn't know. One path represented security; the other, a radical freedom that was both thrilling and terrifying.

The idea for a cross-country ride came from this uncertainty. It was an experiment designed purely for the value of exploration, an attempt to answer a question through experience. It was, in retrospect, my first R&D project. I was investing time not in building a resume, but in building a foundation of character. I was rebelling against what journalist Michael Easter calls the "Comfort Crisis," the phenomenon of our modern lives being so safe and predictable that we've removed the transformative challenges that build resilience. "The comforts and conveniences of modern life are blessings," Easter writes. "But they've also eliminated the need for us to be gritty, tough, and resourceful." On my 3,600-mile bike ride across America, I deliberately injected grit into a life that was threatening to become too comfortable, too soon.

The wildness I encountered on that cross-country ride taught me that innovations often arise from the space and experiences we create outside of our daily obligations. Space outside of our daily norm of hard, dedicated work can break apart the ruts of dull and repetitive designs we too frequently fall into.

Ever since that pivotal journey, to honor the spirit of the ride and combat the inertia of mediocrity, I carve out about ten percent of our company's time for non-client design projects. I want to continue investing in our collective imagination by protecting space for hearing that "call to adventure." Each of us uses this time to explore ideas that fascinate us—from high-density affordable housing for wildfire-ravaged areas to underground greywater reclamation systems. Much of this work only goes as far as the R&D page of our website, but its value isn't in its immediate profitability. It's in the creative muscle it builds. Tuning into these adventurous calls keeps our minds sharp and prevents the procedural, boilerplate work of construction documents from dulling our creative edge.

To chase an idea just to see where it goes, you have to give your team, and yourself, the space to get lost.

The Slow Win

There is a unique kind of mental anguish that comes from riding a bicycle across Nebraska. The road is a straight, black ribbon over a sea of green and gold, stretching to a horizon that never gets closer. The wind across that landscape is like a physical wall, an invisible barrier I pushed against for twelve hours a day. Every day. It was Campbell's "road of trials" in its most monotonous and grueling form. I would pedal furiously, head down, only to look up and see the same grain silo I spotted an hour ago. Progress, I realized then, had to be measured in inches. There was no triumphant "arrival" at the end of a day. My daily victory was simply not quitting.

In his book *Do Hard Things*, coach Steve Magness dissects the nature of true toughness. He argues against the performative, "suck it up" version of grit and advocates for a more grounded, realistic approach. He writes, "Real toughness is experiencing a situation, taking it all in, and then making a calculated decision to proceed. It's clarity and control."

Staring down that Nebraska headwind, there was no room for bravado. I can't pretend it didn't suck—there's nothing like pedaling uphill into the wind for hours upon days. But real toughness didn't involve ignoring the misery; it meant accepting it. *This is the reality of the situation,* I told myself. *The wind is not my fault. I can't control it. I can only control how I pedal.* I learned to stop looking at the horizon to gauge my success and to focus instead on the next telephone pole, the next crack in the pavement. I learned to embrace the grind, to find satisfaction in the relentless, repetitive motion of my legs and feet.

This experience was my first and most brutal lesson in what I now call the *Slow Win*. In business, as in the Plains, moving the best ideas forward often feels like pushing against a wall of indifference, just as discouraging and unending as that headwind. When we began developing solar and battery microgrids for commercial buildings, for example, the logic behind the innovation was undeniable: it saved money, increased property values, and helped the planet. But its adoption rate was agonizingly slow. Moving toward a more solar-powered future felt like pedaling into the wind.

But that's when the lesson from the road kicked in. I knew I had to aim for Slow Wins over arrivals. I couldn't get discouraged by the unchanging horizon. That wouldn't bring it any closer or make the reality of the situation disappear. I had to practice what Magness calls grounded confidence. I had to accept reality: the slow market, the hesitant clients, the frustrating process. Only then could I make a calculated decision to proceed, this time with my focus on the process, not the outcome. That next meeting, the next proposal, the next conversation. I had to keep pedaling, knowing that, eventually, the landscape would change. I had to believe in the Slow Wins, because those wins were the only ones that kept me going.

The Right Tools, The Right Mindset

My breaking point on that bike ride came in late September, somewhere on a desolate stretch of highway between Casper and Shoshoni, in Wyoming. After more than 2,000 grueling miles, my rear tire finally gave up. On that one forsaken day, I blew three back tubes in a few hours. I was out of patches, out of spares, and miles from anything. And the work of fixing those tubes had been tedious and repetitive—flipping the bike, wrestling the tire off the rim, finding the minuscule hole, patching it, and reassembling it all, only to hear that demoralizing *hiss* once again, just minutes later. It was a soul-crushing, inefficient, and profoundly depressing day.

This was definitely the moment when I found myself in "the belly of the whale," as Campbell calls it, the point in the hero's journey where it seems like they've reached total defeat; the hero is metaphorically swallowed, digested, and must be reborn. My ego, the part of me who had it all figured out, died on that greasy roadside. If I had merely performed toughness, I wouldn't have accepted my reality. I would have raged at the sky. But real toughness looked different. It entailed quietly, humbly accepting the facts: my plan was flawed, my equipment had failed, and I could not solve this problem alone. I had to hitchhike into the next town, a humiliating act that was also the only rational path forward. I had to let my old self, the self-reliant hero, die and be reborn as someone pragmatic enough to ask for help, ego be damned.

Lying on that roadside shoulder, I would have killed for a better tool. A smartphone with GPS. A support vehicle. Or, at the very least, a tougher set of tires. I recall that moment to this day because it provides a vivid image of how the design industry currently finds itself, suffocating under the dead weight of its own inefficiency, bloated plan sets, opaque pricing, and byzantine permitting, and ready to kill for a better tool to fix it all. Well, that powerful tool has arrived in the form of artificial intelligence. AI can shred our inefficiencies and reinvigorate our field. The first time I used an AI image generator, it produced four design options in seven seconds, a task that would have taken twenty hours in computer-aided design (CAD). Today's architectural AI is still learning, and if we keep learning alongside it, there's potential to let it handle the "flat tires" of the design industry, freeing up our human creativity to focus on the journey itself—on beauty, function, and solving real human problems—not simply on trudging down the road, empty-handed, in search of a better tool. It's already here, and we just might not be as stranded as we think.

Castles of Sand and the Guardians of the Threshold

Initially, my intent to bike across the country was a castle made of sand—a fragile idea hatched without a complete plan. The first people to challenge it were the ones I respected most: my family. I remember sitting in their living room, the air thick with their concern. To them, my ride seemed like a self-serving publicity stunt.

Their response to my sandcastle was a textbook reaction. In *The Science of Fear*, Daniel Gardner explores the way our brains are wired with two systems of risk assessment: "Head" (rational, analytical) and "Gut" (instinctive, emotional). Gardner writes, "For our ancestors, a strange person, a strange place, a strange situation, these were all potentially dangerous. A cautious, even fearful, response was a good rule for survival." My grandparents' "Gut" was screaming. My plan, a young man traveling alone into the unknown, triggered every ancient alarm bell. The familiar risk of a boring but stable finance job seemed infinitely safer than the unfamiliar, vivid risk of the open road. Their fear wasn't irrational; it was instinctual. Their reaction also fit into Campbell's monomyth, fulfilling the role he called the "guardians of the threshold"—the protectors of the ordinary world who test the hero's resolve.

But to answer the call, you have to move past the guardians.

I listened to their fears, I practiced empathy for their perspective, but I also had to have the courage to disagree. I had to defend my sandcastle.

This experience taught me my first and most critical lesson about innovation: You must have a perspective and the courage to stand by it. This is true even when it comes to your clients. The good ones will respect you when you tell them they're wrong. The ones who don't are not worth your time. Trying to please everyone is a recipe for mediocrity.

This is the mindset you need for true innovation. You need the courage of your convictions to defend your sandcastle from the guardians, but you also need the humility to walk into any room and listen. Justify your ideas with data, but hatch them from a place of creative freedom. Frank Gehry's buildings require proprietary software to be realized, but he makes his first drawings on napkins.

My cross-country journey changed me. It was a voluntary *misogi*, a term Michael Easter borrows from Japanese tradition to describe a transformative ordeal. By pushing my physical and mental limits, I recalibrated my definition of "hard." The discomforts of the business world, a difficult client, a delayed project, a tough negotiation, pale in comparison to biking through a hailstorm in the Nevada desert or having my bike break down in the middle of nowhere.

This shift in perspective is the "elixir" the hero brings back from the unknown world that helps them face the trials of the ordinary world with a new, grounded confidence. It's the courage to build your castles of sand, the wisdom to defend them, and the humility to let the Nevada rain wash them away and start again. That is the heart of innovation.

Chapter 12:

Visibly Valuable

If you ask a group of people to describe their ideal office using only words, these are the ones you will get every single time: Bright. Productive. Quiet. Lively. Colorful. Collaborative. These words are positive, aspirational, and almost completely useless. They're not descriptions of specific needs or requests; they are empty vessels into which each person pours their own private meaning. My "lively" is a space buzzing with spontaneous conversation and energy. Yours might be a room with vibrant art on the walls and plenty of natural light, but God forbid anyone speaks above a whisper. My "productive" is a quiet, isolated pod where I can achieve deep focus. Yours might be a bustling team room where you can pull people into a quick brainstorming session at a moment's notice.

You can't expect someone to describe what they want when they don't possess the specialized language of design. It's like asking a patient to self-diagnose a complex illness; they can tell you where it hurts, but they can't give you the medical terminology. Forcing them to try leads to a Tower of Babel scenario, where everyone is speaking but no one is understood. The common focus group, the corporate brainstorming session—these are the tired rituals we perform in the hope of finding clarity, but they almost always lead to more confusion.

They are destined to fail because of this language barrier. If we want to build spaces that truly work, we have to invent a new language, one that is visual, intuitive, and rooted in authentic human behavior.

The Failure of the Old Guard

Before we can build a new model, though, we must first perform an honest autopsy on the old one. For decades, the design and business worlds have relied on two primary tools for generating ideas: the brainstorm and the focus group. Both are deeply flawed approaches, often doing more harm than good. But what about them, specifically, doesn't lead to the type of feedback that's useful to a future design?

The Brainstorming Illusion

The concept of brainstorming, as formalized by ad executive Alex F. Osborn in his 1953 book *Applied Imagination*, sounds wonderful in theory. Get a group of people together, encourage a high volume of wild ideas, and forbid any and all criticism. The goal of this is to create a safe, uninhibited environment where creative genius can flourish, and brainstorming quickly became the corporate go-to for "unlocking innovation."

The only problem is that it hardly ever works. Almost immediately, academic research began to show that individuals working alone consistently produced more, and better, ideas than a group of people brainstorming together. The reasons for this come from the following elements at play within human psychology: production blocking, social loafing, evaluation apprehension, and dominance and conformity. Each of these elements impacts how we show up to brainstorming sessions or take part in focus groups:

Production blocking

This term describes a simple, logistical fact when brainstorming in a group. Only one person can speak at a time. While you're politely waiting for your turn, that brilliant, fragile idea you had can easily evaporate. You get distracted by someone else's point, you lose your train of thought, or you simply forget. The very structure of these sessions blocks the natural flow of individual thought.

Social loafing

This term describes the diffusion of responsibility that takes place within a group. Individuals often exert less effort when working alongside others than they would when working alone because they can rely on other people's contributions. Essentially, the thought process goes like this: why push myself to come up with a truly unique idea when I can just nod along with what everyone else is saying?

Evaluation apprehension

The "no criticism" rule during brainstorming is a noble fiction. People are social animals, keenly aware of hierarchy and perception. Even without explicit criticism, we fear being judged. This causes us to withhold our truly unconventional or half-formed ideas—the very "wild ideas" these sessions are supposed to encourage—for fear of sounding foolish in front of our peers or, even worse, our boss.

Dominance and conformity

Inevitably, the louder, more extroverted, or more senior members of a group tend to dominate the conversation. Quieter or more junior members, who may have equally valuable insights, hesitate to speak up. This imbalance leads the group to converge on a few popular ideas too quickly, a dangerous phenomenon known as "groupthink."

The result of all these elements at play within our psyches is a brainstorming session that generates a high volume of safe, mediocre ideas that reflect the opinions of the most dominant people in the room. Innovation is performed but not actually generated.

The Focus Group Fallacy

The focus group has an even deeper and more insidious flaw than the brainstorming session. Not only does it fail to generate ideas, but it often produces data that is actively misleading. Originating during World War II as a tool to study propaganda, the focus group was co-opted by the market research industry to understand consumer preferences. Its fatal flaw, however, is that it's built on a complete misunderstanding of human nature: it assumes people know what they want *and* will tell you the truth about it.

In reality, the focus group is a Petri dish for preference falsification, misrepresenting one's own wants or beliefs due to perceived social pressure. What people *say* in a focus group is often a world away from what they actually *do* or *believe*, primarily because of two psychological effects: group dynamics bias, and the observer effect:

Group dynamics bias
  This happens when a single articulate, confident, or high-ranking participant hijacks the entire conversation, swaying the opinion of the group. When this majority sentiment forms, others may be hesitant to voice a dissenting opinion simply to avoid social

friction. The results gathered in this setting don't represent a collection of individual truths but a snapshot of a temporary and artificial group consensus.

The observer effect

The very act of being watched and questioned changes our behavior and our answers. Participants in a focus group are no longer just employees or users; they are performers. They aren't necessarily making choices for themselves, they're making choices based on what they think the boss, the moderator, or their manager wants to hear. Most participants will offer whatever feedback they think will make them look smart, agreeable, or innovative.

Before I started my own architecture firm, my job for about fifteen years was developing a design strategy for large corporations and then finding the right team to execute it. In my early days, I followed the established playbook. I'd watch as famous firms like Gensler or HOK ran their process. It often started with a meeting of company leaders gathering around a wall of curated images, little stickers in hand—green ones went on the images they liked, red ones went on the images they disliked. Then, they were asked to explain their choices.

This, unfortunately, was a useless exercise. Not only were they using ambiguous words ("I like this picture because it feels more "dynamic"), they were also doing this exercise in front of each other, everyone taking turns placing their stickers on the board. The outcome was preordained and predictable. The junior vice president isn't going to put a green sticker on a playful, edgy design if she just saw the conservative CEO put a red one on it. This groupthink exercise did little more than reinforce the aesthetic preferences of the most powerful person in the room, guaranteeing a design that was safe, predictable, and almost certainly wrong for the broader organization.

Better Words and Visual Language

The old methods are clearly broken, so how do we gather the truth about the actual needs and preferences of a company's workforce? The answer lies in the two-pronged approach of Design Democracy: disseminating meticulously crafted narrative surveys and intuitive, engaging visual surveys. The key to both types of surveys is making them accessible, private, and unbiased. No moderators. No group dynamics. Just a direct line to the authentic preferences of each individual.

The Art of the Question

Before we get to the power of visuals, we have to appreciate the science behind asking a good question—the pivotal piece at the heart of a useful survey. The survey as a viable method of gathering information has had its own evolution, moving from simple tallies to precise measurements of human attitudes in all their complexities.

In the 19th century, surveys were blunt instruments for achieving government censuses. These surveys asked factual, direct questions: How many people live here? What is your occupation? The goal of these questions was to get a description of people's situations, not to understand them at a deeper level.

In the 1930s, psychologist Rensis Likert developed his famous scale, which allowed researchers to measure intangible concepts like agreement and satisfaction for the first time. Instead of getting a simple "yes/no" answer from survey participants, researchers could now gauge the *intensity* of a feeling (Strongly Agree, Agree, Neutral, Disagree, Strongly Disagree). This introduced nuance and precision into the data.

From the 1970s onward, the cognitive revolution taught us that the *way* we ask a question dramatically affects the answer. Researchers learned to hunt down and eliminate sources of bias from their surveys as a result of this new discovery. The following biases often plague a sloppy survey, skewing the answers before participants even have the chance to consider their responses: leading questions, double-barreled questions, and ambiguity:

Leading questions

A bad question like "Would you agree that our office desperately needs more collaborative spaces?" is really a statement fishing for confirmation. It doesn't generate an organic, authentic response from survey participants. A good, neutral question along those same lines would be, "How would you rate the current availability of spaces for collaboration?"

Double-barreled questions

A question like, "Do you find the lighting and temperature in the office comfortable and productive?" is impossible to answer accurately. What if the lighting is great but the temperature is terrible? To assess these elements, this question must be split into two separate, focused questions, not lumped together in a double-barreled one.

Ambiguity

"Do you come to the office regularly?" is a meaningless question that will generate meaningless answers simply due to the innate ambiguity within it. "Regularly" could mean once a week to one person and four times a week to another. A better question to assess attendance would be, "In a typical month, how many days do you work from the office?" The more specific you can be with your question, the better.

The goal of these narrative surveys is to make them clear, specific, neutral, and easy for everyone to understand in the same way. We keep them to fewer than twenty questions, which usually takes someone under seven minutes to complete. We never ask for open-ended comments, which are difficult to analyze and often reintroduce the same vague language we're trying to avoid. We even ask the same core question in a few different ways to scrub for interpretation bias. The truth is that if you make your surveys easy, clear, and fast, a huge number of people will tell you the truth about their needs and desires for the new design.

The Visual Revolution: Seeing is Believing

Narrative questions are crucial for understanding workflows and behaviors, but design is visual. It's emotional. It's aesthetic. Expecting people to articulate their spatial needs using only text is like asking someone to describe a symphony using only numbers. This is where visual surveys become our most powerful tool. With a visual survey, we can overcome the limits of language, reduce fatigue and increase engagement, tap into people's emotions and intuition, and generate actionable, specific data.

Overcoming the limits of language

Visuals provide a shared, concrete reference point that eliminates ambiguity. Instead of asking someone what "collaborative" means to them, I can show them three distinct images of team spaces—one has a large table and a whiteboard, one includes a cluster of soft seating, and one features several small, open-walled pods—and ask, "Which of these spaces would best support your team's work?" The image bypasses the linguistic confusion of ambiguous words and individual definitions and gets straight to the participant's intuitive preference.

Reducing fatigue and increasing engagement

It's a chore to respond to a long list of text-based questions. It leads to "survey fatigue," where people get bored and either quit or start randomly clicking through to get it over with. Visuals turn the survey into a more engaging, almost game-like experience. Asking someone to drag and drop icons representing their daily activities (deep focus work, phone calls, team meetings) onto an interactive floor plan is not only more interesting, but it also yields far richer data than a simple written questionnaire.

Tapping into emotion and intuition

Great design is about how a space *feels*, and that feeling is often a gut reaction that's hard to articulate. A visual survey can assess someone's immediate, intuitive reaction to a proposed design by presenting them with the range of material palettes (warm woods versus cool metals), furniture styles, or lighting schemes being considered. This visual presentation taps into survey participants' emotional responses and gets a better sense of how they might experience the new space.

Generating actionable, specific data

"Where do you prefer to work?" is a much less useful question than showing survey participants an image of a workplace environment and asking them to identify where they would feel most productive and least productive in that environment. This type of visual assessment provides a powerful heatmap of the entire office, revealing problem areas and hidden successes that would be far harder to spot in a text-based survey. The result is specific, location-based data that is immediately actionable for designers.

Surveys, and visual surveys in particular, are a fundamentally more democratic way of getting truthful, organization-wide feedback than the more traditional methods of brainstorming sessions and focus groups. Presenting participants with images—often in combination with clearly worded prompts—and assessing their responses to them is a more intuitive process, far less dependent on a person's vocabulary or confidence and far better at capturing the nuanced human experiences at the heart of great design. Private, online surveys allow the design team to gather authentic, consensus-based data from a whole diverse organization about what people really want and need from their environment, not just the responses of people saying what management wants to hear.

Observation, Data, and the Truth

Surveys, both narrative and visual, are essential for understanding what people *think* and *feel*. But to get the full picture, we must also understand what people do, where they walk, and where they actually spend their time. This requires putting on our anthropologist hats, as discussed in Chapter 8, and gathering empirical, observational data to pair with survey results and get a fuller picture of the current problems the new design aims to solve.

Walk the floor on a Tuesday morning and then again on a Thursday afternoon. Spend a day working from a touchdown spot in the office. Watch the invisible choreography of the workplace. Who is actually in the office, and when? Where do people congregate? Where are the dead zones? Who is on the phone all day, and who is camped out coding in a dark corner? Observe where and how meetings actually happen. Do people book a conference room for a quick ten-minute chat, or do they grab an informal space? Watch how people really use the available technology, how they take breaks, and where they eat lunch.

During these observations, look for the things that reveal cultural value. What do people like to do when they're *not* doing their primary work tasks? How do informal meetings differ from more formal ones? What does self-care look like at the office? Which bathrooms get the most use? Asking yourself targeted questions like these as you gather data will help you assess the real centers of activity in an office, as well as determine where a company's culture lives. This is the "ground truth" that provides the essential context for all your survey data.

In addition to qualitative observation, we need quantitative data. The simplest and most effective tool for gathering this is a good old-fashioned security badging study. That will give you solid data about who is in the office, on which days, and for how long, which will further clarify what peak utilization and mobility patterns look like in the space. In environments without security badges, chair sensors can provide even more granular detail about when someone is at their desk and how often they get up and move around the office.

Synthesizing the following three layers of information as part of your design process will give you a rich, three-dimensional model of any organization's culture:

1. What people say (narrative surveys)
2. What people prefer (visual surveys)
3. What people do (observation and hard data)

During this multilayered data-gathering phase, you may encounter what seems like contradictory results. You might find that everyone *says* they want more quiet focus rooms, but the badge and observation data shows that the most popular and vibrant parts of the office are the informal social hubs. While on the surface this may be a confusing finding, it isn't a contradiction; it's a critical insight. It tells you that you need to solve for both of these observations—providing dedicated quiet zones (thus acting on the feedback you gathered in your surveys) while also enhancing the social spaces that are the true heart of your office culture (which you wouldn't have realized without gathering quantitative data).

By seeing the truth, in all its multi-dimensionality, you can finally build the truth.

Chapter 13:

Endurance & Iterations

Let's look at the lesson buried within the grueling, monotonous reality of a solo, 3000-vertical-foot climb up a mountain pass. The lesson has little to do with cycling and everything to do with the nature of accomplishing any truly difficult task. You learn that progress isn't made through grand gestures of inspiration, but through the relentless repetition of a single, simple action—the next pedal stroke. It's a master's thesis on the mental focus required to shrink a monumental challenge down to repeatable, incremental steps. This chapter makes the case that this unique blend of physical endurance and focused, repetitious behavior is the exact same engine required to navigate commercial-scale design and the labyrinths of permitting and development. It's about understanding that the slow, often frustrating process of iteration and repetition are not flaws in the system to be lamented, but the very path to the summit.

In late September 1998, the air near the base of the Tetons felt extra fresh. At 5,600 feet above sea level, the nights I experienced after full days of biking were getting cold, and fast. The thin nylon of my tent, optimized for its low weight, felt like a porous membrane against the growing chill seeping from the ground as it fell from the Milky Way sky. The cheap motels that occasionally broke the nightly monotony of campsites were becoming scarcer as I pedaled deeper into the expanse of the American West. I was spending every day in the middle of nowhere, and the scenic beauty and isolation that surrounded me were beyond words.

As I left the plains of Nebraska and headed into Wyoming, the landscape underwent a dramatic transformation. Nebraska was deceptively challenging, a relentless series of long, rolling inclines against that stiff headwind. But Wyoming was different. Hills quickly give way to mountains.

Most people who ride across the country do so from west to east, leveraging the steady push of the jet stream in their favor. I, in my youthful confidence, had dismissed this as a minor detail. I was wrong. And I was reminded of just how wrong I was with every pedal stroke. Every day I felt more and more like Sisyphus, attempting to push a rock uphill for all eternity.

My route primarily followed Old Post Road 20, a historic artery stretching from Boston to Oregon. In Shoshoni, Wyoming, Route 20 veers north, heading straight for Yellowstone. But I had a different plan in mind—hopefully one with smaller consequences than pedaling against the jet stream. I intended to duck under that massive range to find a lower, more manageable path across the Continental Divide. I'd made this strategic decision earlier in the summer, studying my already worn paper maps laid out across the beach.

Now, the Tetons rose from the plains with a breathtaking abruptness, a sheer wall of granite and ambition. I was approaching the South Pass of the Wind River Range, which my previous calculations suggested was the gentlest and lowest crossing point of the Continental Divide. But "gentle" and "low" are profoundly relative terms. When the valleys themselves are a mile high, nothing is gentle and nothing is low.

Despite my best laid plans, these were days of incredible beauty and demoralizing effort. Days of soaring vistas followed by hours of rain and unrelenting wind. But somewhere on that infinite stretch between Lusk and Douglas, I witnessed something truly magical. During a break in the rain, with no vehicles in sight for miles, the land beside me came alive. A herd of a hundred wild mustangs, running at a full gallop, overtook me along the opposite side of a simple split-rail fence. The sound was thunderous and primal, a symphony of hooves, dust, and raw freedom. It was a fleeting moment of grace in a landscape defined by its harshness, a reminder that wildness and beauty persist in the toughest of places.

Out there, time stretched and compressed in strange ways. The pace of bicycle touring was both a gift and a curse. I moved slowly enough to absorb the subtle shifts in the landscape, the scent of sagebrush after a brief shower, the texture of the asphalt. These were the gifts. But when I found myself a mile above sea level and climbing all day, pedaling stroke after stroke became a sort of forced meditation. As cheesy as it seems in retrospect, I had packed Robert M. Pirsig's *Zen and the Art of Motorcycle Maintenance*, a book that catalogs his cross-country motorcycle trip in order to understand the deeper quality of his experience on the road. "The High Country of the Mind" is Pirsig's metaphor for the realm of rational thought, logic, intellectual analysis, and abstract ideas that we can explore just like any physical journey through actual mountain ranges. I found myself thinking along similar lines the longer I traveled, the further I went.

In my first few weeks on the road, I had the comfort of staying with friends as I passed through Massachusetts, upstate New York, and Ohio. But for the subsequent eight weeks, I was utterly alone. The solitude was an immense, echoing chamber, filled with the rhythmic whir of my chain and the constant dialogue inside my own head. I had ample time to reflect on the college experience I had just left behind and ample time to ponder the seemingly infinite, unwritten future I was riding toward.

And with that reflection came regret.

It crept in during the long climbs, a nagging counter-rhythm to my pedaling. I felt I hadn't leaned into the academic experience enough. Had I taken the right courses? Had I wasted my summers? Why hadn't I spent more time at professors' office hours, or listened more closely to my advisor? Why did I take so many writing classes? What was I thinking, signing up for a wines class? The questions churned, creating a narrative of missed opportunities. I was adrift in a sea of "if onlys." *If only I had majored in something more practical*, I chided myself. *If only I had networked more effectively. If only I had planned my future with more precision.*

It's funny to look back on those thoughts now. My college experience was perfect. I missed nothing. Those writing classes taught me how to communicate, a skill more valuable than any technical course I could've taken. That wines class gave me credibility in social situations, and countless stories too. But I am profoundly grateful for that period of reflection on my ride and for the journals I filled with my anxieties.

The quiet, difficult time I spent wrestling with regret as I pedaled endlessly toward the Continental Divide was a powerful transitional tool. It wasn't a sign of failure; it was the self-powered engine propelling me to capitalize on the opportunities ahead, ones that would eventually lead to great success.

The Productive Power of "If Only"

Author Daniel Pink, in his book *The Power of Regret*, argues that this emotion, which our culture so often tells us to avoid ("No regrets!"), is actually a fundamental, useful, and unavoidable part of the human experience. When we confront it honestly, regret becomes a powerful catalyst for making better decisions, improving performance, and achieving a deeper sense of meaning throughout our lives.

Pink distinguishes between two types of ways we think about alternative scenarios playing out in our lives. The first is "at least" thinking. If you get into a car accident, you might say, "Well, *at least* I wasn't seriously injured." This reframing helps us feel better in the short term. The second type is "if only" thinking: "*If only* I had left five minutes earlier." This tends to make us feel worse initially, as it focuses on a path not taken that could have led to a better outcome.

But here's the crucial insight: while the "at least" people may feel better short term, it's the "if only" people who learn more in the long run. The sting of "if only" forces us to analyze our mistakes, to deconstruct our decisions, and to create a mental blueprint for how to act differently in the future. It's a cognitive tool for iteration.

This is the very essence of the iterative design process. Every architectural project is a series of "if only" moments. "*If only* we had identified this clash in the MEP drawings earlier." "*If only* the client had mentioned their desire for a flexible auditorium during the programming phase." These moments are frustrating, but they are also invaluable learning experiences. They sharpen our skills, refine our processes, and make the next project better.

Working within a consensus-based system like Design Democracy is a strategic way to mitigate the negative impact of these moments. By bringing more voices into the process early and often, we front-load the discovery phase, turning potentially costly late-stage "if onlys" into productive early-stage "what ifs." This collaborative approach doesn't eliminate regret, but it does channel its energy into proactive iteration rather than reactive repair.

Upward Gravity

The day after my encounter with the mustangs was all grit. My map showed what was in store for me: a 34-mile ride from Lander to

South Pass. It looked manageable on paper. It was anything but. The ride took me from 5,700 feet to 8,500 feet above sea level, a single, unrelenting, eight-and-a-half-hour climb. My average speed was a miserable four miles per hour.

My bicycle and gear weighed a combined sixty pounds. On a long, steep grade, that weight didn't just feel heavy; it felt like an active force pulling me back down the mountain. Each pedal stroke was a victory as my world shrank to the few feet of asphalt in front of my wheel and the burning in my legs.

When I finally crested the pass, relief flooded through me. And there, like a beacon of hope, was the Rock Shop Inn. I don't know what I would have done if it wasn't there or hadn't been open that day. I was fully smoked and wanted nothing more than a hearty meal and a real bed. I walked into the restaurant, its bar stools and neon signs like a dream, and ordered myself a beer and steak. Then I checked into one of the simple cabins out back, ate another 2000-calorie dinner, and slept for the next eleven hours.

The Quagmire of Modern Permitting

That bicycle climb is the single best metaphor I know for navigating the modern real estate development process. The project itself is the journey. The regulations, the bureaucracy, the unforeseen obstacles, that's the extra gravity. And the process itself is a slow, grueling, iterative climb where your average speed feels agonizingly slow.

Complex projects with multiple buildings, interior spaces, outdoor patios, and intricate landscaping are the norm. If you try to permit everything at once, you risk getting bogged down in a bureaucratic nightmare. Even with sophisticated design teams and strong general contractors, the process is ultimately at the mercy of building departments, their plan checkers, and their inspectors.

Here is the single most disruptive fact in real estate today: municipalities, their building departments, and their inspectors can interpret the code any way they want, and they can take as much time as they want to do so. There are rarely consequences for them and no incentives to move faster.

This problem varies according to state, county, and local jurisdictions, not to mention federal influences. Entitlement and permitting in Texas and Florida have fewer steps and take about half the time as they do in California. Yes, I love my hometown of Santa Monica, CA. But when I designed and built my own place in Santa Monica, a 3,100-square-foot home finally completed in 2022, the plan-check process took 632 days and cost $77,000 in fees before I was issued a permit. No construction project of any size should take that much time to permit or cost that much per square foot.

California leads the nation on innovation of all kinds. We lead the nation on environmental protections, and we lead the nation on government overreach. But California is in desperate need of a massive permitting and entitlement process overhaul. The current system is a tangled mess of overlapping jurisdictions and "one at a time" steps. Cities outsource plan reviews, adding extra costs. Resubmissions are often handled by different individuals, leading to a complete loss of project continuity. A simple application for new electrical service from the Los Angeles Department of Water and Power (LADWP) must navigate seventeen sequential departments. The average time for this process is 400 days. An LADWP senior official once admitted to me that during that 400-day period, a submission is actively being reviewed for a total of only twenty-one days. The rest of the time, it's just sitting in a queue.

My office employs people whose primary job is simply following up with plan checkers. It can take months and dozens of emails just to get a single reply. The system is fundamentally broken.

AI, Incremental Decisions, and Slow Wins

If ever there was an opportunity for artificial intelligence to provide immediate, transformative value, it is in the municipal plan-checking process. We already use AI-powered tools to help us draft plans that are compliant with building codes. It is logical to use the same technology on the review side. An AI could scan a set of drawings and check for compliance with national, state, and local codes in minutes, not months or years.

This process wouldn't replace human plan checkers. It would free them from the monotonous, mind-numbing task of line-by-line code checking and allow them to focus on what humans do best: handling edge cases, considering requests for variances, and applying nuanced judgment. Imagine if the existing workforce became twenty times more efficient. The logjam would break.

But until that day comes, we must solve this painful problem by layering the phasing of our permit submission strategy, embracing the incremental progress we achieve, and celebrating our Slow Wins along the way.

The Wedbush headquarters in Pasadena is a perfect case study of this layering approach to permitting, and it's described in more detail in Case Study 6 in the Appendix. The project, still currently underway, involved renovating the top two floors of the city's tallest building. The scope included the interior offices and a large outdoor patio on the penthouse floor. My project design team and I could have submitted this as a single permit package, which would've entailed fewer drawing costs and lower plan-check fees. But we knew better. The "extra gravity" of permitting an outdoor structure on a high-rise would have held the entire project back.

Instead, we split the project into two phases. Phase one was the interior, a relatively straightforward process that took about ninety days to permit. Phase two was the outdoor patio. Once we finished the interior work of phase one, the client was able to move in and operate their business in their beautiful new space. Meanwhile, the permit for the phase-two patio emerged from plan check after 541 days and six rounds of comments. This outdoor area was a much smaller project in comparison to the interior. Not much more than furniture with shade canopies. Over the course of the review process, the design for the shade canopies didn't undergo substantial changes since our first submission. Yet each round of review, often done by a different person, introduced new, minor requests that reset the clock.

By splitting the permits, we broke the project into increments. The cost of doing so was negligible compared to the alternative: a 541-day delay on the *entire* project. Reflecting on this now, breaking the permitting into two phases was one of my greatest contributions to the project. I had to lean into the architect's role of translator and strategist. My job was to be the bridge between design and the client's vision on one side, and the technical language of our specifications and the hard data we collected through our Design Democracy process on the other side. We had to bridge that gap, translating our expertise and the client's vision into a compliant, buildable reality.

Design and its ugly subset of permitting activities is a complex terrain to navigate. Making it through the permitting process is a long, slow climb against headwinds and extra gravity. It requires patience, persistence, and a deep well of resilience. You must find meaning in the struggle and have the wisdom to break an impossibly long journey into a series of manageable, incremental steps. You must celebrate the Slow Wins, because they are the fuel that will get you to the summit.

Case Study:
The "We'll Take It from Here" Fallacy—This is the part of the journey where the plan on paper meets the messy reality of the climb. It demands a

specific kind of process grit—the ability to keep moving forward, to achieve small, iterative Slow Wins even when the path is unclear. Technical expertise alone is not enough to get you through. We saw this with a utility-scale energy developer in a project that inspired me to articulate what I call the "We'll Take It from Here" Fallacy. Their team was filled with brilliant engineers who were technically superior to us in every way, yet they were culturally paralyzed by their fear of uncertainty. They had the engine, but they lacked the endurance for the race, and their projects stalled completely until we could help them break the logjam. It's a powerful reminder that the most critical skill in any project is often the courage to navigate ambiguity. (See Case Study 3 in Appendix A.)

Chapter 14:

Tough Empathy

My team and I have this client. For the sake of this story, let's call them "Helpful Health." They are a large healthcare provider for underserved communities with special needs, and they are, without exaggeration, some of the best people we've ever worked with. Their mission is clear, their team is passionate, and they are a rare combination of decisive and kind. We genuinely enjoy going out of our way for them. So, long before they committed to the building for their newest primary care facility, we were already working to get ahead of the planning.

The process of getting ahead often begins with a simple, standard request: we ask the building owner for the "as-built" drawings. These are the architectural plans that define the existing condition of the space. Having these drawings makes it infinitely easier and faster to design exam rooms, offices, and waiting areas. It also eliminates the re-creation of the restroom and path-of-travel drawings required by every building department for permitting. Getting these "as-built" drawings is standard practice and the foundational first step of many projects.

The landlord for Helpful Health gave us none of these drawings. That's not an entirely uncommon scenario, but it was the first tremor of the earthquake of incompetence that followed. This landlord, it turned out, became the newest addition to our "blacklist" of commercial real estate slumlords. They dragged their feet on everything. Simple approvals took weeks. Straight answers were a foreign language. They met all of their contractual responsibilities with delays and excuses. And they were nearly a year overdue on paying our client a million dollars in tenant improvement allowances, money they're contractually obligated to provide.

This landlord is both a perfect case study in how a bad actor can poison a project, and the perfect backdrop for demonstrating the profound value of two of the most potent tools in our Design Democracy process: meticulous documentation paired with the philosophy I call *Tough Empathy*. Case Study 5 goes into more detail about our experience with Helpful Health.

Indisputable Project Records

The lease for the Helpful Health deal was thin on specifics: the timing of the landlord's responsibilities, the precise mechanics of how money would be exchanged, and the triggers for when rent would commence. None of these elements were nailed down. In the end, the only thing that protected our client from this landlord's malicious apathy was the extensive notes and the follow-up email documentation my team created after every single meeting, every phone call, and every interaction.

This experience reinforced what I already knew: the importance of meticulous documentation.

Every time I bring a new project manager onto my team, I give them "the lecture" on the vital importance of meeting minutes. And every time, I see that familiar look in their eyes—a millennial skepticism. They think this kind of old-school documentation is boring, outdated, and a colossal waste of time.

Then, a few weeks later, it happens. A contractor, a consultant, or, in the case of Helpful Health, a landlord, says the inevitable words: "That's not what we agreed to." And like the sword of justice, the meeting notes come out. We forward an email with the date, the attendees, and the precise action items agreed upon. In ninety-nine percent of cases, the issue evaporates instantly. In longer cases, it might take weeks and the involvement of lawyers to resolve, but the side that almost always wins is the side with the better notes. The argument dissolves in the face of the written record.

This is why my team and I don't just take notes; we create an indisputable project record, a running, real-time log of the project's life, documenting every decision, commitment, and change made throughout its lifecycle. It is not a "gotcha" paper trail; it's a catalogue to reference any time faulty memory, miscommunication, or outright dishonesty threatens to overshadow the clarity we've previously gained. It's a way to decrease the friction of these very natural impediments.

This is one of the most immediate and practical applications of artificial intelligence in our field. AI-powered contextual notetakers are a game-changer when it comes to these indisputable project records. Dozens of tools can now transcribe entire meetings, identify different speakers, and generate concise, actionable summaries. This technology has made our meeting minutes clearer, more accurate, and more objective than ever before. There are far fewer scrappy fights about who committed to what when there is essentially a full-time digital court stenographer in every meeting. The AI creates a neutral third-party record, turning potential conflicts into simple matters of fact-checking.

For our project with Helpful Health, this written record was the instrument of truth we needed. Every time the landlord claimed ignorance about an approval deadline or tried to renege on a verbal commitment, we had the documentation to hold them accountable.

They were never going to be pleasant to work with, but having this real-time project log clearly organized and at our fingertips forced them to honor their commitments, however grudgingly.

Tough Empathy: The War Against Apathy

Keeping meticulous records as a way to solve problems and disputes during a project is certainly a proactive approach. But the best project leaders take it even further. They don't just solve problems; they prevent them. This requires moving beyond simple project management and into the realm of Tough Empathy.

I emphasize empathy, character, and compassion throughout this book because I truly believe that the more we challenge ourselves physically and intellectually, the better we become at embodying these virtues and the better our designs will be. And there is a corollary to this: the deeper we dive into challenging ourselves, the more finely tuned our bullshit detector becomes. We develop the ability to see clearly when others are purposefully shirking their responsibilities, and to call them out on it.

Tough Empathy is tough love for the professional world. It's a declaration of war against laziness, apathy, and mediocrity. Too often, we see consultants, designers, and contractors whine about deadlines, complain about requests for cost-saving alternatives, or mope when asked to try harder to find competitive pricing. But these tasks are at the heart of their roles and an indisputable part of a healthy design process. Apathy like this only hurts the field and diminishes the success of design as a whole. It doesn't even serve those who are avoiding their tasks—it just draws out the process.

I developed Tough Empathy by immersing myself in a variety of jobs and volunteering experiences throughout my career. I learned what it takes to complete a task. I can call bullshit on how much time it takes to frame a wall because I've framed walls before. I can call bullshit on the cost of wiring an outlet because I've wired outlets. I can call bullshit on a timeline for a set of construction drawings because I've spent countless weeks producing them myself. Conversely, I can understand deeply the challenges of this work too. Very often, I've launched into creating a custom door and its frame or building millwork, only to learn that it's much more difficult than it looks and that the professionals only make it look easy because they have been doing it forever. Tough Empathy goes both ways.

I recommend spending time on a real jobsite, and not just walking around in a clean hard hat taking notes. This is the single fastest way to dismantle your own design privilege. If you're already deep into your career following business school or decades into your design practice, there's still time. Take a week off, confront the discomfort, and volunteer. Ask a general contractor if you can shadow a superintendent. This is your "dojo," your "ring." Offer to do the work: take out the trash, sweep the floor, cut studs, run conduit. Get your hands on the materials so you can viscerally understand how hard these tasks are, how much process grit they require, and how much time they truly take. This isn't about becoming a master carpenter; it's about building the *empathy* side of Tough Empathy, so when you lead, you are doing it from a place of earned respect, not theoretical privilege.

This isn't about being an expert in every trade. It's about knowing enough to ask the right questions, questions that demonstrate you understand the basic components of the work. It's also about earning the respect of your team by showing that you appreciate their craft and their challenges. When you can ask a subcontractor a specific, informed question about their means and methods, it changes the entire dynamic. You are no longer just a manager pushing for a deadline; you are a knowledgeable partner in the process. The questions themselves—clear, direct, and rooted in reality—cut to the heart of what's real and encourage everyone to exert their best effort.

Sometimes, though, you'll encounter people who are not your partners. You will deal with the industrial-grade privilege and entitlement discussed earlier. And here, Tough Empathy requires a different tactic: radical patience.

It may be some landlord broker who has been steadily failing upwards for decades. He's made just enough money to think he knows what he's talking about, but very little of it is grounded in reality. In your first conversation together, he starts with mansplaining basic concepts, then postulates on all the reasons you won't need permits in his building, all while never providing the information you actually need. It is tempting in these moments to dismantle their porous logic and expose their incompetence. But doing so—while satisfying for a few fleeting minutes—is a waste of time and energy because it slows everything down in the long run.

Tough Empathy in situations like these requires accurately diagnosing what's taking place. You are likely dealing with someone who has been insulated from accountability their entire career. The bar is incredibly low as a result. In some cases, and for some roles, there's no special education required, no rigorous apprenticeship process, no real licensing to speak of—just a history of taking people to lunch and giving out firm handshakes. Tough Empathy in this context means accepting someone's professional limitations and communicating with them with clear, simple, one-step-at-a-time instructions. That, and documenting everything.

Fighting Your Way into the Documents

Let's look at the key parts of the design and construction process that *must* be incorporated into the commercial leasing and purchasing transaction documents. There are some vital conversations that must happen early on in these brokerage transactions, as there are whole projects won or lost before a single wall is ever drawn. The architectural and construction implications of the lease or purchasing agreements can have multi-million-dollar consequences. The good brokers will bring you and your client's attorney into the loop on draft leases or purchase agreements from day one. The bad brokers will try to keep you out, seeing your involvement as a complication, and you will have to fight your way into these conversations. Your client must also insist that you are there.

Once you're in the room, there are several critical exhibits and clauses you must scrutinize and shape: the as-built drawings, the base building definition, the construction rules and regulations, the landlord review timelines, the commencement of rent, and the disbursement of tenant improvement allowance. Since each of these affects the lasting success (or failure) of a project before it even begins, let's go through them in more detail so you know exactly what you're asking for and why.

1. As-Built Drawings

At the start of every project, you must get the as-built drawings of the building you're working with. Any resistance to providing these is a major red flag. If they don't exist, the landlord or seller must be made responsible for commissioning a new set of these drawings. This isn't just a convenience; these drawings are a legal requirement for any project to go through plan check. For the last thirty years, it has been standard practice for the architect and/or general contractor to submit digital as-built drawings to the building owner upon project completion. So, the landlord had these drawings at some point.

But what usually happens when you ask for these drawings is a ridiculous dance between you and the landlord. You'll ask, they'll refuse. The attorneys will get involved and agree that the documents should, indeed, exist. The landlord still claims they can't find them. The attorneys then agree that the landlord should bear the cost of creating new ones. Miraculously, this is the point when the drawings often appear. As soon as the landlord might have to spend a single dollar re-creating documents they already possess, they suddenly find the twenty minutes needed to search their virtual plan room.

Your Mandate: Ensure the transaction documents legally require the asset owner to provide accurate, up-to-date as-built drawings and site surveys within a week of the transaction close. If the landlord doesn't provide them in this amount of time, there should be an additional landlord-provided allowance for money and time defined for the tenant's architect to produce.

2. Base Building Definition

This document, typically an exhibit to the lease, should be a simple, 1,000-word description of the asset's condition prior to your renovations. This document includes critical information: How much electrical power is available? What is the heating and cooling capacity? Are the elevators operational and code-compliant? Is the building compliant with the Americans with Disabilities Act (ADA)?

A landlord's resistance to defining these things is, at best, lazy. At worst, it is a deliberate attempt to avoid responsibility for providing information about the basic, functional systems that make a building fully functional.

Your Mandate: Insist on a detailed "Base Building" exhibit that narratively defines the delivery condition and performance requirements of the asset, from its HVAC capacity to its ADA compliance.

3. Construction Rules and Regulations

Paying attention to these might seem pedantic, but the building's construction rules can hide enormous costs. While clauses like "no smoking on site" are easy to agree to, other statements can have big consequences. Pay close attention to the allowed hours of operation. It's reasonable to require loud or smelly work (like demolition or painting) to be done after hours. It is *not* reasonable to require *all* work to be done at night, which can nearly double your labor costs. Look for unreasonable requirements around trash removal and restroom use, too. If you can't use the landlord's dumpster, you'll incur extra costs for daily debris removal. And if your workers are forbidden from using restrooms on an occupied floor, you'll have to pay for indoor porta-potties—which are as gross as they sound.

Your Mandate: Have your architect and contractor review the building's rules and regulations before the lease is signed. Understand the operational constraints and their cost implications.

4. Landlord Review Timelines

If you are leasing space, the landlord will, reasonably, want approval rights over your plans. But these rights must be bound by strict timelines. Although it may seem obvious that there would be a shared urgency to plan review, it doesn't always work that way. Without a defined timeline, this review period can become an unrestricted risk and a huge drain on energy, so make sure they're in place. Five business days for the landlord to review plans at the end of the schematic design phase is a reasonable timeline. Another five-day review when you submit plans for your permit is also standard. This gives them a chance to coordinate your proposed work with the building's core systems.

Your Mandate: The lease must specify the exact number of days the landlord has for each plan review. It should also state that if no comment is received within that timeframe, the plans are deemed approved.

5. Commencement of Rent

This is one of the most financially critical clauses. The landlord wants you to start paying rent as soon as possible. But you should only start paying rent when you can actually use the space. In a world where permit times are wildly unpredictable, committing to a fixed start date is incredibly risky. We have had many clients who were forced to pay rent on a space that was still a hard-hat construction zone because they signed a lease with a bad rent commencement clause.

Your Mandate: The language must state that rent commences on "the later of [a specific target date] OR [a certain number of days after the certificate of occupancy is issued]." The word "later" is crucial. If the clause says "the earlier of," you have a huge problem. Tie the start of rent to the project's completion, not to a date on a calendar.

6. Disbursement of Tenant Improvement (TI) Allowance

Many leases include a TI allowance, where the landlord contributes a certain amount of money per square foot toward your construction. But be wary of a "turn-key" offer where the landlord builds the space for you; you will get a cheap, cookie-cutter result. So, don't accept it. You need to control your own design and construction.

Accordingly, you need to control the flow of the TI allowance. The lease *must* define the milestones for allowance disbursement. We've had two recent projects where the timing was left undefined, and

the tenants didn't receive a dime until long after the projects were complete. They were forced to front the entire construction cost, which was a huge cash-flow burden.

There are two good ways to structure the TI allowance:

Chunks
> The allowance is disbursed in three or four equal parts at key construction milestones (e.g., at the start of construction, the halfway point, and substantial completion).

Monthly proportional reimbursement
> For larger projects, you can submit monthly reimbursement requests. If the TI allowance covers fifty percent of the total project cost, then for every $100,000 contractor invoice you pay, you submit it to the landlord for a $50,000 reimbursement.

Your Mandate: Ensure the lease has a clear, defined schedule for the TI allowance disbursement so that the money flows predictably throughout the construction process.

Good contracts are not separate from the design process; they are a part of it. Narrative documents that accompany the drawn material will guarantee better collaboration and efficiency, allowing more time and effort to be focused on the quality of the design.

Fair and detailed contract documents provide the guidance, clarity, and accountability that keep a project on the rails. They are tools to troubleshoot problems before they arise, and they lay the foundation for any Tough Empathy you may need to use ahead.

Case Studies:
The High Cost of a Low Price—Insisting on a fair contract and a qualified team isn't about padding a budget; it's about mitigating risk. Our client

learned this the hard way. They signed a terrible lease and then, against our advice, hired a "one-man-band" contractor who promised to build their studio for half the market rate. After six months of delays and a mountain of change orders, they ended up paying exactly what we would have charged, but lost a fortune in rent on an empty space. This is the inevitable result of chasing an unrealistic number instead of predictable value. (See Case Study 4 in Appendix A.)

The Indisputable Project Record—Every time I bring someone new onto the team, I teach them about the value of notes and minutes…And then a few weeks later, they see the value when it saves their skin. Like clockwork, someone says, "That's not what we agreed to," and, like the sword of justice, the meeting notes come out, and the whole issue usually goes away. We saw the power of this firsthand on a project for the healthcare provider we've been calling "Helpful Health." The case study goes into more detail about the story of our work together. (See Case Study 5 in Appendix A.)

Chapter 15:

Completing the Circle

Our culture is obsessed with metrics. The desire for measuring ourselves against others (and ourselves) is woven into the fabric of our culture: standardized tests in school, statistics in sports, titles and promotions in corporate America. Testing is measuring, and there is no other way to get better than first knowing where you stand.

But there is no more lightly measured group than designers, and the few measurements that are in place don't challenge the status quo. When it comes to institutional architecture, a building is almost exclusively measured by two metrics: the cost to design it and the cost to construct it. Its actual performance—its efficacy at helping its occupants succeed—is almost never part of the equation. Considering the immense expense of every single project, this lack of measurement is the equivalent of professional malpractice. Testing ongoing performance is actually written into the American Institute of Architects' (AIA) recommended practices as a post-occupancy evaluation (POE), yet it's the first thing to be discarded from the field. No one values this recommendation, so it doesn't happen.

What if this were different? What if we truly valued the actual performance of architecture? The outcome of upholding a standard, and of measuring projects against that standard, would likely have the same effect it has everywhere else: revolutionary change within the industry, projects pushed beyond their previous limits, successful design from start to finish—and after.

Think Moneyball for buildings. We are still in the pre-Moneyball era of architecture. Project teams are still being picked based on glossy magazine photos and the charisma of the lead designer—or by how good they look in their uniforms.

Remember *Moneyball*? The movie chronicles the story of how the Oakland A's general manager, Billy Beane, built a winning baseball team on a shoestring budget. He rejected the old-school intuition of scouts and embraced a data-driven strategy instead. Of course, an inevitable clash between gut feeling and empirical analysis ensues. But Beane and his assistant used statistics to find undervalued players, focusing on metrics like on-base percentage instead of conventional measures of talent like a "good swing." This allowed the A's to outthink, rather than outspend, their competition.

This is the future of our practice. This is the true vision and process of Design Democracy. We use data about people, their movements, and their goals to create spaces that demonstrably lead to more successful individuals and higher-performing organizations. The AIA's POE recommendations are lofty and commendable, but they often focus on qualitative metrics like thermal comfort and air quality. These things are important, but they don't mean a damn thing to the C-suite if the building isn't also a financial success. Winning in baseball and winning in design—both are tied to the bottom line.

The same Design Democracy methodology that creates success at the beginning of a project continues at the end of a project and beyond. The visual and narrative surveys that gather input at the start of a project become the template for post-occupancy evaluation as well. By asking the same questions and comparing the "before" and "after" data, the Design Democracy circle completes itself. When we had unfettered access to data at Newmark, we were able to prove that the direct results of our work yielded higher office attendance and higher per-person revenue. The data was unequivocal.

Completing the circle isn't an extra step; it's the final, critical arc of the process itself. By building the follow-up with workplace users into the schedule and the contracts from day one, it becomes an effortless and integrated part of the project's life. It's not disruptive, it's not costly, and it provides the proof that our work is an investment with a measurable return.

The Phantom Fumes: Managing the Unmeasurable

But even with perfect, Moneyball-style data, it's not easy to get started in the Design Democracy process. Even Billy Beane was met with stiff resistance. We are dealing with human beings in all their complex, emotional, and sometimes irrational glory. We can design the most statistically perfect space in the world, and some people will still be unhappy.

In 2006, I was working for Studley in downtown LA, starting to make real money and build a track record. The head of the region, Mark, asked me to get the office repainted. It was a beautiful space with an incredible art collection, but it was starting to show its age after a decade. I scheduled the specialized art movers and the painters, and then I wrote a series of emails notifying my colleagues of the work that would happen over the weekend and that they might notice a faint smell on Monday morning. I assured them the paint was low-VOC—the stuff that makes paint smell.

Then, an "emergency in the art moving world" forced the movers to reschedule. I scrambled to cancel the painters but forgot to send a follow-up email to the office, notifying them of the delay. As far as my colleagues knew, the office was still being painted over the weekend. No big deal, I thought. We'll do it later.

Then came Monday morning. Three people complained of fumes. Two had to go home early with extreme, fume-related headaches... from a nonexistent paint job.

As humans, we have a deep-seated fear of change. My team and I find that in any major project involving a move, thirty to forty percent of survey responders express some kind of anxiety about the new space. Confronting this fear is central to the design process.

Interestingly, however, people hired within a few months after a company has moved into their new space express almost no complaints. For them, the new office isn't a change; it's just a part of their new job. The space is a source of comfort, not anxiety.

This is where the power of Design Democracy kicks in; we're not just collecting data for data's sake. Consensus, even if it's just a simple majority, is our primary tool for managing fear. The process of being heard—narratively and visually—is calming. The process of having the survey results discussed clearly and openly is reassuring. When the people who will be using the new space are informed partners in the process, it is healthier for them and immeasurably better for the final design.

Why Measurement Fails

So, if we have the tools to measure the performance of a design project, why does this so rarely happen? Because organizations are plagued by institutional biases and priorities that prevent them from measuring what truly matters. Each motive and bias originates from a different place, but the outcome is the same: the results that could inform the field of architecture and move it forward get overlooked.

Corporations: The Efficiency Trap

Corporations are the most likely to embrace measurement as a tool for gauging the success or failure of a design project, but they are also the most likely to measure the wrong things. As we saw in Chapter 6, the cubicle was a revolutionary concept that originally promoted collaboration, but under the control of big corporations, this innovation warped from their relentless drive for spatial efficiency until it became the soul-sucking box we know today. Corporations can take a good idea too far, optimizing for cost per square foot while ignoring its devastating cost to culture and productivity.

Philanthropies: The Frugality Theater

Nonprofits are often so focused on the public's perception of their frugality that they fail to study the actual impact of their work. They don't want to appear to be wasting donor money on "nice" things like post-project surveys or success metrics. In the design projects my team and I have done for nonprofits, too many of them underspend on critical systems like restrooms while overspending on flashy task chairs, because a fancy chair signals "we value our employees" while good plumbing is invisible. Their measurements are frequently skewed by optics, not outcomes.

Government: The Process Quagmire

Government offices can become so obsessed with the perceived fairness of their procurement processes that they lose sight of the actual quality of a design. Marc J. Dunkelman's *Why Nothing Works*, tells the story of an ice rink project in 1980s New York City. To prevent overspending, the city prohibited a single general contractor, forcing the city to hold prime contracts with every single sub-trade. What they gained in transparency, they lost tenfold in coordination. Costs ballooned, and the project ground to a halt. Then a certain famous real estate developer offered to do it for eighty percent less with guaranteed performance and cost. He got it done.

Dunkelman argues that the problem when it comes to moving government processes forward is a "vetocracy," where countless groups have the power to say "no" to a project but almost no one has the authority to say "yes." To complete the circle of the Design Democracy process and actually measure what matters, we need to streamline permits, accept that progress involves trade-offs, and restore legitimate authority to empowered leaders. Leaders who wield their authority with the tools of Design Democracy will then be putting the voice of the people to work for the good of the people.

The Choice: Creator vs. Critic

Ultimately, completing the circle of the Design Democracy process is a choice. It is a choice about what kind of person you want to be: someone who listens to new ideas, empathizes with others, and creates innovative designs, or someone who staunchly believes in tradition alone, remains stuck in their privilege, and chooses templates over the fear of the unknown. The first one creates; the second one criticizes.

There is a certain kind of wisdom in being consistently suspicious of new ideas. But it's not a wisdom that builds or discovers, it's one that stays fixed in self-preservation. It is the wisdom of a ship that never leaves harbor; it can never sink, but it will never discover new lands either. This mindset operates on a simple, seductive principle: you can never be faulted for a failure you didn't endorse.

The critic cloaks themself in pessimism, hoping that will keep them safe from errant ideas. It's easy to poke holes in a new approach; the critic can simply lean back, list obstacles, and forecast failure, creating an aura of seasoned intelligence. By saying "That will never work," critics absolve themselves of all risk. If an idea fails, they are a prophet. If it succeeds, their critique is forgotten. They lose nothing.

That is the safe harbor of the sidelines. That is the path of least resistance. It is also the path to irrelevance.

The creator, meanwhile, must be vulnerable, hopeful, and willing to be wrong. The creator is ready to be tested, to be measured. They understand that embracing regret means learning from mistakes, not avoiding them. Creators, empowered by a deep and empathetic connection to the people they serve, are those who will build our future, not just react to it.

History remembers the creators, the builders, and the risk-takers. The critics, for all their "correctness" about the inevitable failures on our way toward innovation, are ultimately just a footnote in the story of progress.

Completing the circle of Design Democracy, then, involves far more than a post-occupancy evaluation. It requires commitment: commitment to the continuous cycle of listening, creating, testing, and iterating. Commitment to choosing, again and again, the vulnerability of the creator over the safety of the critic.

Case Study:
The $250,000 Slow Win—This is the essence of a Predictive Placemaking strategy: it's not about finding the cheapest option, but the one that offers the highest probability of success. A perfect example is a financial services client who faced a significant schedule risk from custom-fabricated materials. We advised them to make a painful but strategic upfront investment of $250,000 to split their permits. That single move saved them from a year-long delay that would have cost them millions. They didn't buy the cheapest plan; they invested in the winningest one. (See Case Study 6 in Appendix A.)

Chapter 16:

The Architecture of Courage

The seeds of Design Democracy took root on a journey. My bike ride across the country at the beginning of my career took me face-to-face with regret and fear, and it led me to embrace the difficulty of the unknown. That journey continued to grow and shape me long after I reached the coast and packed up my bike for home. It became a metaphor for the choices I continue to face every day, and the choices that face all of us. Will we allow the fear of failure and regret to trap us in the critic's safe harbor? Or will we choose the creator's path and venture into unknown horizons?

Confronting fear is the common denominator of all meaningful growth, whether you take a bicycle trip through Wyoming, right into a demoralizing headwind, or whether you're in a boardroom trying to champion a design that defies convention. Fear presents itself as the seductive voice of the critic, urging us to take the easier path: turn back, choose the safer, templated design. The fear of the unknown road is no different from the professional's fear of a budget overrun or the failure of a bold new idea. But the path through fear is also the same: you keep moving forward into discomfort, moving through it, knowing that the greatest resistance often precedes the most spectacular view.

This is the journey where true empathy is forged, facing our fears out on the road or inside the boardroom. The easy path is remaining stuck in a position of design privilege, comfortable as a successful architect from a prestigious university, and calmly discussing designing for others while knowing nothing about their wants and needs. But designing for true success remains an abstract concept until we, ourselves, have been stripped of that privilege. Until we are simply a person in need, until we confront our own physical and emotional limits, until we understand vulnerability from the inside out, we will remain limited in our perspective and, in turn, our profession. To truly be successful in design, we must transform empathy from something we imagine into something we remember.

This hard-won empathy becomes the most powerful tool in our designer's kit. We'll no longer be designing from a safe distance because we'll have felt exactly what the occupants of a space feel at the start of a big change: disoriented, stressed, or powerless. But if we design from this starting line, and if we incorporate the principles of Design Democracy every step of the way, then we design with a different kind of purpose. We now understand that a well-designed space is not just about its visual appeal; it's about creating psychological safety, reducing friction, and anticipating human needs. This visceral understanding and where it leads—seeking out the "missing voices" and designing for the "stress cases," not just the idealized user—is the momentum that drives Design Democracy. It is the heart and soul of the process, and it is what I strive to cultivate in my team.

I want my team and I to be immersed in the ongoing process of facing our fears and developing empathy for our partners, clients, and colleagues. To foster this, I have everyone on my team spend time on the jobsite, in the building department, and in client meetings. They might just take one measurement, deliver a set of plans, or simply sit and take notes, but the process of being there and getting outside their usual confines is invaluable. Of course, I still fantasize about putting my entire design team on a framing crew for a week, but even getting them to experience these alternate realities for a day or two enhances their visceral connection between a drawn concept and the rough tolerances of the real world. Far more important than fostering unique and clean drawings, I want to create leaders who can see through the dogma of tradition, listen to those who are hurting, feel the pain of an unsolved dilemma, and solve problems with empathy and ingenuity combined.

When we share the struggles of others in our work, we open what I can only describe as a two-way empathy portal. We hear them, and they hear us. But we can only open this portal when we're unafraid of hearing what someone else needs—really needs—from our design. By confronting our own fears and limitations, we develop this deeper understanding of others. And when we lead from that place of earned vulnerability, the people around us begin to understand us at a deeper level too, creating a virtuous cycle of trust and collaboration, which ultimately leads to better, more successful designs.

A Challenge to Everyone

The principles of Design Democracy offer anyone who dares to use them a formidable business strategy. For too long, the design of our buildings has been treated as a capital expense to be minimized. But this is a profound and costly misunderstanding. When we instead embrace an inclusive, data-driven design process, we are forging a powerful tool for companies to attract talent, unlock productivity, and foster a resilient culture. Maintaining the traditional, top-down approach to design, on the other hand, is the equivalent of taking an enormous gamble on the intuition of a select few. The Design Democracy process de-risks that investment by eliminating the waste of preference falsification and creating an environment that catalyzes human potential, rather than containing it.

This brings us to a final call to action—a challenge to everyone who has a stake in the spaces we share.

To the architects and designers: I urge you to abandon the myth of the lone genius. Your greatest value lies not in the singularity of your vision but in your ability to listen, translate, and facilitate the collective wisdom of others. Trade the safety of the critic for the vulnerability of the creator.

To organization leaders: Your workplace is far more than real estate; it is the physical embodiment of your company's culture. Stop restricting its creation and start wielding it as the strategic tool it is. Have the courage to trust your people and to invest in a process that will reveal the authentic, cultural DNA of your organization.

And to every person who uses these spaces: Recognize that your experience is valuable data. Your voice matters. Your daily frictions and small joys are the critical insights upon which great design is built. Demand to be heard.

The future of design is not in the hands of a privileged few but in the collective action of us all.

So, let's get a little uncomfortable. Let's design through struggle, confront our fears, and generate understanding. Let's find what we're afraid of and train ourselves to transform those fears into our biggest strengths. Let's build the empathy muscles that create better leaders, better projects, and a new world of design, where compassion comes first and the bottom line shows it.

Appendix A:

Case Studies

Case Study 1: A Cautionary Tale of Design Privilege

The energy, productivity, and presence of the people design is meant to serve is the true measure of its success. But what happens when that success metric is ignored? This case study demonstrates just that.

The Story: Design Privilege on Steroids

We were brought into a project for a prominent apparel brand in the usual way: late. The lease was already signed, key architectural decisions had already been made, and multiple design teams were actively engaged. While my team and I can often overcome the obstacles that a late start brings to a project, this project's structural flaws proved insurmountable.

The setup was a masterclass in fragmentation. Three separate, well-known architecture firms were involved: one hired by the landlord for the historic exterior, a second hired by the landlord for a new interior mezzanine, and a third hired by our client, the tenant, for the final space planning. Our firm was engaged by the tenant to perform project management, with the goal of coordinating these siloed teams. From the beginning, however, it was clear that collaboration was not on anyone's real agenda.

Design privilege was running rampant through this project. The company's CEO had a strong, singular vision for the space. The three acclaimed architecture firms each had their own powerful, ego-driven design sensibilities. When we proposed implementing our Design Democracy consensus-building system to gather input from the employees who would actually use the space, the idea was summarily dismissed. The vision would continue to be dictated from the top down.

Our role was reduced to the bare minimum of design and construction coordination. We delivered the project on budget and on schedule, and the result was, by all aesthetic measures, a masterpiece. It photographed beautifully. We had successfully stitched together the disparate visions of the client and the three architects into what looked like a cohesive and masterful design. High ceilings, asymmetrical windows, sand-blasted historic surfaces, and reclaimed wood finishes all came together in a perfect blend of the coolest industry trends. Magazine worthy to the max.

The space was designed to accommodate 300 people. Yet, in the eight years since its completion, the average daily occupancy has been around 30 people. Despite an initial surge of interest in the new space, attendance fell off a cliff. The COVID-19 pandemic certainly contributed, but even after its effects waned, the office remained a beautiful, empty vessel.

The Analysis: The Cost of an Insulated Vision

So, what happened? By all aesthetic accounts, the design was a success. But, measured by actual attendance and use, it was a catastrophic failure, and the reason for that failure is devastatingly simple: not a single person who was meant to spend their working life in that space was consulted on its design. The CEO and the three architects barely communicated with each other, let alone with any of the department heads or employees.

This project was a massive investment based entirely on the intuition and aesthetic preferences of a few powerful individuals, with zero data from the actual end users—the opposite of the Predictive Placemaking approach of Design Democracy. The project team focused on the "brightest stars"—the CEO and the famous designers—and completely ignored the "stardust of innovation" that lay scattered among the 300 employees. The space they built stood as a monument to the *idea* of the company, but it certainly wasn't a functional home for its actual *culture*.

The Takeaway: An Empty Building Is a Failed Building

This project stands as a stark reminder that design is not a spectator sport or a magazine spread. A project can meet its budget, adhere to its schedule, and win awards, and still be an absolute failure. Without a process rooted in Enterprise-Level Empathy, without a willingness to moderate privilege and listen to the collective voice, designers risk creating a beautiful void.

The ultimate measure of a building's success is not its architectural purity but its human vitality. An empty building, no matter how perfectly designed, is a failed building.

Case Study 2: The Power of Listening

The Premise: Overcoming the Commodity Mindset
One of the greatest challenges we face in our work is convincing potential clients that architecture and project management are not commodities you can take or leave, like the gallon of milk you didn't plan to get on your grocery run but figured might come in handy. There is a deep-seated and widespread misunderstanding that our services are something to be procured at the lowest price *after* the big decisions have been made. But the truth is that our greatest value is delivered *before* the deal is done, by embedding design strategy into the transaction itself.

The Story: A Process that Mirrored a Culture
This story is about a project we were part of for a large and powerful nonprofit we'll call "Pacific Way." It's the story of how we overcame that mindset and proved the immense value of establishing a true partnership with us from the beginning.

At 80,000 square feet, this project would be one of the largest nonprofit headquarters in Southern California in recent years. Initially, the client was hesitant to engage us early. When we explained the core tenets of Design Democracy, however, they had a profound realization: the process we were describing mirrored their own organizational values. They were dedicated to listening, empathy, and accessibility, and they understood the intrinsic power of a methodology built on guided, democratic consensus.

This alignment secured our involvement, and we immediately deployed our survey system. Over the course of the project, we conducted more than ten distinct surveys, each one getting more granular. We began by asking broad questions about work styles and macro ideas of culture. We then honed in on specifics, like desired office frequency and the primary activities people would perform on-site. Finally, we drilled down to the smallest details, using visual surveys to select the most preferred ergonomic task chair.

The Analysis: The Curb Cut Effect in Action

The results of this deep listening process exceeded the client's expectations and provided a powerful illustration of Evidence-Based Empathy.

First, the quantitative success of our Design Democracy process was staggering. In their new headquarters, the average daily occupancy was six times higher than it had been in their previous space—a direct, measurable result of having created a space that precisely aligned with the authentic needs of its users. Furthermore, our detailed analysis of their spatial requirements allowed them to avoid taking additional immediate space, a move that would have been costly enough to kill the entire transaction.

Second, the project was the ultimate manifestation of the curb cut effect, the principle that a design feature created to help a specific group (like a curb cut for those with wheelchairs) ends up benefiting everyone (people with strollers, travelers with luggage, delivery drivers). By engaging in a deeply inclusive design process and listening to a wide array of voices, Pacific Way created a space that was not only more accessible for a few but fundamentally more functional, comfortable, and desirable for *everyone*.

The Takeaway: The Intrinsic Value of Being Heard

The most profound success of that project was the trust and confidence it generated, not just the data we gathered. Because the employees coauthored the design, they felt confident and invested in the project from day one. Even when the final space included elements they didn't personally vote for, they understood and respected the outcome; they knew they had been part of a fair and transparent democratic process. They had been heard. This project demonstrated that Design Democracy is more than a process for building better buildings; it is a framework for building stronger, more cohesive, and more resilient cultures.

Case Study 3: The "We'll Take It from Here" Fallacy

Our energy division specializes in complex projects like microgrids and system upgrades for large-scale clients. In this case study, I describe a time when we worked with a utility-scale energy developer, a client with a deep bench of in-house engineers and construction managers. On paper, their expertise should have made our job easier. In reality, their professional culture, forged in the risk-averse world of public utilities, became the project's single greatest obstacle.

These professionals were immersed in a culture with no incentive for urgency and a deep-seated aversion to the risks inherent in private-sector development. This led to what I call "analysis and management paralysis"—an inability to take the necessary incremental decision and documentation steps with partial but majority consensus. They lacked the muscle memory for confronting the fear of uncertainty, an essential skill for moving a project from concept to construction.

The Story: An Overconfident Takeover

We were engaged on two separate projects to lead the initial schematic design, entitlement, and permitting processes. Both were proceeding on track. As we navigated the complex path toward permit issuance, the client, confident in their in-house team's technical knowledge, made a fateful decision. "We'll take it from here," they proclaimed.

But this was expertise privilege in action. They believed their engineering prowess would be sufficient to shepherd the project through its final, most nuanced stages. We offered our Tough Empathy in the form of a gentle warning, advising that critical subtleties in the process could easily trip them up. But they declined our offer of continued support, and we moved on to other work with them.

Months later, we received urgent calls. Both projects were dead in the water. The client's team had become entangled in the very issues we had predicted. Critical permits were never obtained, mandatory inspections were missed, and crucial ADA-compliant access assemblies had been ignored in the design. They had the technical knowledge but lacked the process-based grit to execute, and the project suffered as a result.

The Analysis: The Last Mile Is a Human Mile

Our team was able to save the day by immediately reengaging with the regulatory bodies on a human level. We leveraged our longstanding relationships, created and submitted the missing documentation, and arranged for the missed inspections and corrective work. The core of our client's failure to move through these components, and our success, came down to three things:

Paralysis vs. Slow Wins

The client's team was frozen by their fear of making a mistake. They were unable to achieve the small, iterative Slow Wins required to maintain momentum toward the end goal. Our team broke that logjam by tackling one small, manageable problem at a time—something we had trained for time and again by flexing our muscle of confronting uncertainty head-on.

Process blindness vs. process respect

The client's team viewed permitting as a technical requirement to be checked off a list. We viewed it as a dynamic process built on relationships, communication, and a deep respect for the perspectives of the regulators. This empathetic approach allowed us to untangle the mess collaboratively rather than confrontationally.

Technical skill vs. human contact
Our client's engineers were brilliant on paper, but they failed because they did not engage in the hands-on, human-to-human contact required to navigate the final stages of inspection and approval.

The Takeaway: Process Grit Is an Expertise in Itself

In the end, we were able to save our client millions of dollars and shave a full year off the revised activation schedule. This case study is a powerful reminder that technical expertise is not a substitute for process expertise. The final, most critical mile of any complex project is often not about engineering prowess; it is about navigating a complex web of human interactions, regulatory nuances, and unavoidable uncertainties with empathy and persistence. The ability to confront the fear of this ambiguity and execute with decisive, empathetic action is a discipline in itself—and it is often the one that makes all the difference in the success or failure of a project.

Case Study 4: The High Cost of a Low Price

The Premise: A Flawed Foundation

A successful project is built on a foundation of trust and a clear, fair contractual agreement. When that foundation is cracked from the beginning, no amount of skill or effort can prevent a compromised structure. This is the story of a project where a series of well-intentioned but misguided decisions—made before we ever entered the picture—created delays, frustrations, and unnecessary costs down the line.

The Story: The Siren Song of an Unrealistic Number

We were brought into the deal too late to ensure a steady foundation from the start. The clients had already signed a "terrible lease" that lacked any of the standard protections for a tenant. There was no base building definition and no work letter defining construction protocols, leaving them entirely at the mercy of the landlord's mood. Most critically, the rent commencement was tied to an inflexible and imminent date, a classic mistake that forced the tenant to pay for months of rent on a space they could not yet occupy. This flawed legal foundation set the stage for the conflict to come.

The initial design challenges were significant, involving the conversion of a foreign designer's metric-based vision to comply with California's Imperial measurements and the labyrinthine ADA codes. The larger challenge, however, was the client's unshakeable conviction that the project could be built for half of the market rate.

Our firm, acting as the executive architect and project manager, provided a comprehensive design-build proposal based on our experience and a realistic understanding of the client's high-end tastes. They rejected our construction price and insisted on finding a general contractor who would meet their number. This is the flip side of design privilege: a client so convinced of their own budget assumptions that they reject the market expertise they're paying for.

They felt vindicated when they found a contractor whose bid matched their unrealistic target. Our due diligence, an act of Tough Empathy to protect the client from their own optimism, revealed a proposal that was grossly underinsured, misunderstood in its scope, and lacking critical details. After a month wasted on this failed candidate, the client found another "one-man-band" contractor willing to agree to their price.

The project was already behind schedule, and the real chaos was just about to begin.

The low-price contractor immediately began generating change order after change order, recouping his costs on every item that wasn't explicitly detailed in the flawed proposal. The client's own indecisiveness compounded this merry-go-round, with each change of their mind creating yet another opportunity for an upcharge from their "one-man-band" contractor. Almost immediately, the project fell even more behind schedule. The contractor then took a two-month hiatus for personal reasons, followed by another month off.

After six months of delays and a mountain of change orders, the final construction cost was exactly what we would have charged the client in the first place. The client, however, paid a much higher price: an additional six months of rent on an unoccupied space, and the immense stress of a chaotic and unpredictable process.

The Analysis: The Illusion of Savings vs. the Reality of Value

This scenario demonstrates what can happen in lieu of Design Democracy's Predictive Placemaking strategy. Instead of evaluating the overall value and predictable outcome of partnering with an experienced and properly capitalized firm, the client chose to prioritize the lowest initial bid—a seductive but ultimately meaningless statistic. A better approach to their design process would have been recognizing that our proposal, while having a higher sticker price upfront, represented the de-risked, most probable path to success. The cheap bid from the "low-percentage player" was statistically destined for failure.

The Takeaway: Trust Is the Ultimate Currency

The cheapest bid is often the most expensive choice in the long run. This case study is a stark reminder that the true value an experienced firm provides is not just in its design or construction skill, but in its ability to anticipate challenges, price them honestly, and navigate a project to a predictable conclusion. The upfront investment in a fair contract and a qualified team is the single best insurance a client can get against the far greater costs of delays, change orders, and a chaotic process, as well as no indisputable project record to stand by when communications go awry. Ultimately, the most valuable and cost-effective asset on any project is trust in who you're working with—and you want them to be your expert partners, not just the cheapest option.

Case Study 5: The Indisputable Project Record

This is a case study about a common but challenging adversary: the dysfunctional landlord. Our client, a primary care provider we refer to as "Helpful Health" in Chapter 14, engaged our team early as the design-builder, which was a significant advantage in shaping the project toward success. However, that advantage was immediately compromised by a flawed lease, signed without architectural review, that put our client at the mercy of a landlord who was, by every measure, incompetent, unhelpful, and bent on obstructing progress. The owners were absent, their property management was rude, and their third-party project manager was grossly underqualified. This landlord's standard practice was to control all construction for their tenants, and their inexperience with a tenant-controlled process manifested as anxiety, resistance, and a pattern of bad-faith delays. Having an indisputable project record was the key factor that enabled us to get fair recompense for our client.

The Story: A War of Attrition by Documentation

The core conflict of this project arose from the landlord's refusal to disburse the tenant improvement allowance. The lease was vague on timing, and the landlord weaponized this ambiguity to withhold funds until the very end, creating a significant cash-flow burden on our client. This became the first battle in a long war of attrition, a war we were only able to win because of one critical, nonnegotiable piece of the Design Democracy process: the indisputable project record. From day one, we started documenting every interaction, every conversation, and every agreement, which meant we had a record of the landlord's every broken promise.

This meticulous record became our primary tool for creating leverage in three key areas:

Failure to provide as-builts

The landlord never provided the contractually required "as-built" drawings and was unclear about the specifications of their own building's HVAC systems. When the system predictably underperformed upon activation, they attempted to blame our design. Our clear documentation proved that the failure was a direct result of their insufficient information on the system, shifting the responsibility and cost back where it belonged.

Unpermitted work and Americans with Disabilities Act (ADA) access

The landlord was contractually obligated to provide an ADA-compliant exterior walkway. After initial resistance, they undertook the work themselves. In a stunning display of design privilege, they bypassed the same municipal permitting process they required of us. We documented their failure to submit plans or obtain permits, creating a clear record of their negligence that became a powerful negotiating tool for rent concessions.

The abandoned return air issue

The landlord insisted on routing changes to our mechanical design that ultimately caused significant air circulation performance issues. They then refused to provide any collaborative help to untangle the problem they had created. This is where our team's Tough Empathy came into play. We deployed an investigative "strike team" of technicians to perform the hands-on diagnostics the landlord refused to do, solving the problem with our own expertise and decisive corrective action.

The Analysis: Documentation as the Ultimate Strategic Weapon

A well-documented process can overcome almost any dysfunctional partnership. The landlord's entire strategy was based on creating ambiguity and plausible deniability throughout the process of working with us. Our strategy was to counter that ambiguity with relentless clarity. Every documented failure incrementally built our client's case and shifted the power dynamic. Our hands-on site investigations protected the project's integrity through direct, difficult, and necessary action. And our indisputable project record ultimately transformed every potential "he said, she said" argument into a matter of objective fact—the ultimate defense against a bad-faith actor.

The Takeaway: Your Best Defense Is a Disciplined Process

In the end, our client received everything they were owed and more, precisely because our documentation left the landlord with no room to maneuver or evade their responsibilities. This case study is a stark reminder of two core principles: First and most importantly, always have an architect and an attorney review your transaction documents before you sign them. The cost of a few hours of expert review is infinitesimal compared to the cost of a flawed lease. Second, a disciplined, meticulously documented process is not a bureaucratic chore; it is your single most powerful strategic weapon in navigating the inevitable challenges of any complex project.

Case Study 6: The $250,000 Slow Win

While many of our case studies begin with our team being brought in late to mitigate damage, this is a story of what's possible when we are engaged at the right time. The project for this client, a financial services firm, came from an experienced brokerage team, one who understood the critical importance of layering in architectural, project management, and legal expertise during the earliest phases of site selection and lease negotiation. This client valued a world-class team and, even more importantly, listened to their advice. This created the foundation for a process built on trust and proactive, strategic decision-making.

The Story: The Trellis Gambit

The Wedbush Headquarters project was a jewelbox penthouse headquarters on the top floor of the tallest building in town, complete with a wrap-around rooftop deck. The client and their architecture firm embraced the principles of Design Democracy, consistently pushing for consensus and incorporating feedback from both group leaders and staff to ensure the design would be well-loved and well-used. However, the high-end nature of the project presented significant logistical risks, particularly in its extended lead times for custom finishes.

My team, charged with protecting the budget and schedule, identified one item as a major threat to that goal: the large, outdoor pergola trellis assemblies, which were being engineered and fabricated in Europe during a time of widely fluctuating tariffs. Based on our experience with foreign vendors and the city's notoriously rigorous permitting for rooftop structures, we predicted a high probability of significant delays.

This is where we had to practice Tough Empathy. We advised the client to make a difficult, counterintuitive decision: to proactively anticipate these delays and separate the permit process for the exterior terrace from the main interior project so the whole project wouldn't grind to a complete halt if our predictions were correct. This decision would instantly add $250,000 to the budget in additional drawings, city fees, and expediting costs. It was a painful, upfront cost, but we argued it was the best insurance against a potential catastrophe. The client listened and trusted our advice.

What we suspected was exactly what happened. The worst-case scenario unfolded with the trellis as the city required a complex wind-load study before proceeding with the design. The foreign vendor struggled to provide the necessary calculations. Obtaining shop drawings became nearly impossible. The pergolas, and the entire terrace project, were delayed by almost a full year. But because of our early strategic decision, the much larger and more critical interior headquarters project was completely insulated from the chaos.

The Analysis: A Predictive Placemaking Move and the Ultimate Slow Win

The decision to spend $250,000 to split the permits is the quintessential approach of Slow Wins. It was an unglamorous, strategically defensive, and costly move that produced no immediate result. Yet, it was the single most important project decision, saving the client from a one-year delay on their entire headquarters—a delay that would have cost more than ten times the upfront investment in rent, productivity, and momentum.

This was a pure Predictive Placemaking strategy in action. We used our experience and historical permit data to identify a high-probability, high-impact risk within the plan. We then made a calculated process investment to neutralize that risk entirely. It was a move based on a clear-eyed assessment of the most probable outcome, and we ended up saving the client loads of stress and money by putting Tough Empathy into action.

The Takeaway: A Proactive Strategy Is the Best Insurance

The client's new headquarters is a testament to the power of bringing the right team in early and trusting their expertise, even when their advice is difficult to hear. The willingness to make smart, strategic, and sometimes costly upfront investments is what separates the most successful projects from the ones mired in delays and unforeseen costs. True risk mitigation isn't a line item; it's a strategic mindset and proactive decisions.

Appendix B:

The Design Democracy Playbook

The traditional tools for gathering design input—focus groups, town halls, and open-ended questionnaires—invite ambiguous feedback and create a stage for only the loudest voices to be heard. Additionally, they are Petri dishes for preference falsification, where participants say what they think they *should* want rather than what they actually need. To build a feedback system rooted in truth, we need a better instrument.

The Survey System: From Ambiguous Opinions to Actionable Data

The Design Democracy survey system is just that instrument. It is a three-part, data-gathering and analysis engine designed to bypass the limits of language and the pressures of group dynamics. By using a strictly multiple-choice format in our surveys and augmenting our analysis with artificial intelligence, we generate clean, quantifiable data that reveals the authentic cultural DNA of an organization. This is the practical foundation of Evidence-Based Empathy.

The Three-Part Survey System: The Engine of Design Democracy

The three-part system—the narrative survey, visual survey, and AI-powered analysis—is the engine of Design Democracy. It is a rigorous, repeatable process for gathering the evidence necessary to de-risk a multi-million dollar investment and create a space that truly reflects its people. The AI acts as a powerful telescope, allowing us to see the entire constellation of an organization's culture, not just the brightest few stars. But the ultimate value of this system is not just the data it produces. It's the act of engaging people in a structured and respectful way, gathering both their insight and their trust. The Design Democracy process transforms a workforce of anxious critics into a team of engaged creators, giving them the agency to shape their future environment.

The Design Democracy Playbook

Part 1: The Narrative Survey—Decoding How People Work

Objective: To capture a clear, statistical snapshot of an organization's various work styles, functional needs, and ideal office usage patterns.

Methodology & Best Practices:
1. **Keep it Concise (Follow the 20/7 Rule).** Limit the narrative survey to a maximum of 20 questions. The entire survey engagement experience, from logging in, giving feedback, and submitting the survey, should take participants no more than seven minutes to complete. This 20/7 rule maximizes participation rates and ensures respondents remain focused.

2. **Multiple Choice Is Mandatory.** A multiple-choice format is nonnegotiable, as it provides clean, quantifiable data that immediately reveals patterns. It's ideal for the analysis that comes next.
3. **Focus on Behaviors, Not Aspirations.** Avoid asking participants vague, aspirational questions. Ask instead about specific, observable behaviors.
   - **Instead of:** "Is deep focus important to your work?"
   - **Ask:** "In a typical week, how many hours do you need for individual, uninterrupted work?" (A) 0-5 hours (B) 6-10 hours (C) 11-15 hours (D) 16+ hours
4. **Triangulate Key Data Points.** Asking a single question per data point can only provide so much information. For especially important metrics, ask a core question in a few different ways to get a richer understanding of the issue.

Part 2: The Visual Survey—Translating Feelings into Form

Objective: To bypass the ambiguity of language ("lively," "modern") and capture participants' intuitive reactions to aesthetics, materiality, and spatial function.

Methodology & Best Practices:
1. **Follow the Rule of Four.** Always present images in a four-quadrant format to provide meaningful variety without overwhelming the respondent.
2. **Isolate One Variable.** This is the most critical part of a visual survey. Each set of four images should test a single, specific design concept (e.g., materiality, lighting, level of enclosure) while keeping all other elements as consistent as possible.

3. **Use a Clear, Simple Prompt.** The question accompanying the images should be direct and focused on feeling or function.
   - "Which of these environments feels most energizing?"
   - "Which of these workstation styles would best support your individual work?"
4. **Start Broad, Then Narrow Down.** Structure the visual survey to move from assessing the general aesthetic (the overall vibe of a space) to assessing the specific details (the type of functional spaces needed).

Part 3: Analyzing the Data—Augmenting Insight with Artificial Intelligence

Objective: To move beyond simple percentages and uncover the deeper, often hidden patterns and correlations within the data at speed and scale.

Methodology & Best Practices:
1. **Use an AI Analysis Tool to Spot Pattern Recognition at Scale:** Feed the anonymized, quantitative data from both the narrative and visual surveys into an AI analysis tool. While a human can spot obvious trends, AI can instantly cross-reference thousands of data points to find nonobvious correlations—the true "stardust of innovation."
2. **Identify Hidden Personas.** Use AI-powered cluster analysis to identify data-driven "personas." The AI can group respondents based on their combined answers, revealing distinct workstyle profiles you would never have found otherwise (e.g., "The Quiet Collaborator" who needs focused team spaces, or "The Mobile Anchor" who needs a flexible but consistent home base).

3. **Cross-Reference Visual and Narrative Data.** This is where the magic happens. For example, the AI might tell you that the group of people who overwhelmingly chose the "biophilic, nature-inspired" aesthetic (visual data) are the same people who spend over fifteen hours a week on "individual, uninterrupted work" (narrative data). Powerful, actionable insights like these will emerge, and they can prove useful for things like designing their specific workstations.
4. **Interpret Data Through the Human Lens.** AI is a powerful tool, but it's not a replacement for the designer. The AI provides the *what* (the data patterns), but the experienced strategist provides the *so what* (the design interpretation). Your role is to ask the AI the right questions and translate its findings into a coherent Cultural Blueprint, turning raw data into a soulful and strategic design.

Appendix C:

A Brief History of Empathy
The Cornerstone of Design Democracy

The word "empathy" is the cornerstone of Design Democracy. It is a fundamentally human ability that, when harnessed at an organizational scale, serves as the ultimate antidote to design privilege. Understanding both its meaning and origin reveals the precise mechanism by which we can build better spaces and more resilient cultures moving forward, and the history of the word itself provides a blueprint for its application.

Part 1: The Two Facets of Empathy

Contemporary researchers have distinguished two critical types of empathy, both of which are essential to the practice of Design Democracy:

Affective empathy
This is the visceral, emotional side of empathy—the sensations and feelings we get in response to someone else's emotions. It is the gut-level experience of mirroring other people's joy or suffering. This is the "feeling" part of empathy, the raw human connection that reminds us we are part of a shared experience.

Cognitive empathy (perspective taking)
This is the intellectual, strategic side of empathy—the ability to identify, understand, and articulate another person's emotions, thought processes, and perspective. This is the "understanding" part of empathy. It is a skill that can be trained, scaled, and systematically applied. Cognitive empathy is the engine of Enterprise-Level Empathy and the foundation of Evidence-Based Empathy; it is the discipline of seeing the world through a thousand different eyes, not just our own.

Part 2: The Origin Story—from Art to Psychology

The English word "empathy" is a relatively recent invention, with a fascinating history that traces back to German philosophy and Ancient Greek culture.

Ancient roots
Our modern word "empathy" stems from the Ancient Greek word *"empathia,"* which comes from the root words *"en"* (meaning "in") and *"pathos"* (meaning "feeling" or "suffering"). At the time of its origin, it meant experiencing passion or a state of deep emotion.

German translation
The direct source for our English word "empathy" is the 19th-century German term *"Einfühlung,"* which literally translates to "feeling into." This concept was first used in aesthetics to describe the act of a viewer projecting their own consciousness and feelings *into* an object of art or nature. An observer wouldn't just look at a majestic mountain; they would "feel into" it, experiencing its sense of rising power and permanence. This

is a perfect parallel for what an architect must do: "feel into" a space on behalf of its future occupants.

Psychological shift
The German psychologist Theodor Lipps later adapted the word and meaning of *"Einfühlung"* to the field of psychology to describe our ability to appreciate the emotional state of another person.

Part 3: The Cornell Connection

The word "empathy" officially entered the English language in 1909. It was coined by the British-born psychologist Edward Bradford Titchener, who was seeking a direct English translation for the German word *"Einfühlung."* At the time he introduced the word, Titchener was a distinguished professor at Cornell University.

Learning this fact was a personally powerful, full-circle moment for me. As a graduate of Cornell's College of Architecture, Art, and Planning, I unknowingly walked the same grounds where the central concept of my life's work was given its English name. The university that provided the foundation for my career is the intellectual birthplace of the very word that best describes the solution to our industry's deepest problems.

From Feeling to a Deliberate Framework

Knowing the history of the word "empathy" reveals its true power. It is both a profound, innate feeling (*pathos*) and a deliberate, intellectual act of "feeling into" another's perspective (*Einfühlung*). To be a truly effective designer, we cannot exist without the multifaceted nature of empathy. Design Democracy provides a framework that honors the duality of both affective empathy and cognitive empathy. It creates a system that respects the raw human feelings of an organization while simultaneously providing the disciplined, cognitive tools needed to translate those feelings into a coherent, actionable, and truly empathetic design.

Appendix D:

Survey Examples

Acknowledgements

An English major friend told me years ago that you shouldn't write a book unless you "have to" write a book. I woke up at 3:30 a.m. on a random day in September of 2024, and I knew: I had to write *this* book. The first thing I did later that morning, after creating the initial two-page outline, was show it to my wife, Amanda. She thought the nascent idea was "interesting," which, as I've learned, is a very high bar. The book would evolve greatly from that early morning, but I was off to a good start.

My parents and my family have always been supportive of the different directions I went. My mom, in particular, would always encourage us to, "dare to be different." My father, a banker who I believe should have been an architect, gave me my first carpentry lessons, my first taste of the "jobsite logic" that would come to define so much of my philosophy.

At the Dedham Country Day School, a shop teacher named Paul Patriarca taught me how to *make* things: a baseball bat on a lathe, a wooden kayak, how to fix an internal combustion engine. He taught me the logic of materials and the grit needed to make things. At that same school, Patrick Tynan taught me about Latin, algebra, and the importance of having a spine.

At St. George's School, Tom Evans taught biology, but more importantly, he taught the *process* of learning. John Scott gave us *Moby Dick* and a window into our own humanity. Tim Richards, my squash coach, was a great and early influence on leadership.

At Cornell, my advisor, Zevi Blum, taught us the foundational rule: draw "what you see, not what you know." This book is, in many ways, an attempt to apply that same principle to architecture.

From Kelly Givens and Stacy Wilder at Studley, I learned how to run teams, how to win, and the critical importance of documenting everything. They are the ones who forged my raw ideas into a professional practice and made me into an Architect.

To my friends and book club partners: surfing and reading books with you might just help us all live forever.

To my Karate teachers, Vassie Naidoo and Jamie Duggan: thank you for teaching me how to truly Confront Fear.

Thank you to my publishing team: Amelia Forsczak for the early guidance and shaping; Carmen Smith for editing; Liz Wheeler for proofreading and indexing; Ramesh Kumar for the formatting, and Isabella Quintes for the cover design that so perfectly captured the book's spirit.

A profound thank you to everyone at my firm, Design Build Labs. This book is a reflection of the work we do together. A special thanks to Maria Rios, who, as always, has a critical hand in everything.

And finally, a special thanks to everyone I have ever worked with: clients, consultants, contractors, and partners. The minute-to-minute realities of every project—the good, the bad, and the gritty—are the Stardust of Innovation for this book, and for my life.

Index

A
Action Office 83
affective empathy 199, 202
ambiguity 115, 129, 130, 144, 179, 185, 187, 195
as-built drawings 151, 152
authenticity 11, 78, 80, 93

B
belly of the whale (Campbell) 120
Big Data 80
Burolandschaft or "office landscape" 83

C
cognitive empathy 200, 202
Comfort Crisis (Michael Easter) 10, 117
compassion 92, 93, 98, 148, 168
confronting fear 5, 11, 47, 116, 165
creator vs. the critic 162
cubicles 1, 84
Cultural Blueprint 197
curb cut effect 41, 98, 174

D
deep listening 27, 33, 61, 174
De-Risking Design 167, 194
design privilege ix, xii, xiii, 1, 7, 17, 18, 20, 21, 34, 40, 47, 149, 166, 169, 182, 186, 199, 207
dominance and conformity 124, 125
double-barreled questions 129

E
Efficiency Trap 160
Einfühlung 200, 201
elixir (Campbell) 122
Enterprise-Level Empathy xiii, 2, 13, 96, 97, 98, 102, 171, 200
evaluation apprehension 124, 125
Evidence-Based Empathy 45, 109, 174, 193, 200
expertise privilege 21, 177

F
Frugality Theater 161

G

grounded confidence (Magness) 119
group dynamics bias 126
guardians of the threshold (Campbell) 121

H

Head vs. Gut (Daniel Gardner) 121
hero's journey (Campbell) 120
human interaction 1, 61, 62, 65, 69, 71, 89

I

impostor syndrome 76
indisputable project record 146, 147, 156, 183, 185, 187

L

leading questions 129
Likert scale 128

M

Middle Management Trap 39, 44, 46, 47
misogi (Michael Easter) 122
Moneyball (for buildings) 158

O

observer effect 126, 127

P

pattern language 61, 62
phantom fumes 159
physical comfort 61, 62, 63, 65, 69, 89
post-occupancy evaluations 157, 158, 163
Predictive Placemaking xiii, 2, 28, 41, 47, 163, 171, 183, 190, 191
preference falsification (Timur Kuran) 104
privilege problem 94
process blindness 178
process expertise 179
process grit 144, 149, 179
process investment 191
Process Quagmire 161
process respect 178
production blocking 124, 125

Q

"Quality Without a Name" (Alexander) 61

R

radical patience 150
real toughness (Magness) 118
regret (Daniel Pink) 138
road of trials (Campbell) 118

S

sandcastle 121, 122
self-care 61, 62, 67, 69, 89, 133
Slow Win 2, 118, 119, 142, 143, 144, 163, 178, 189, 190
social loafing 124, 125
stardust of innovation 23, 33, 34, 40, 44, 45, 171, 196, 206

T

Taylor 82, 87
tenant improvement allowance 146, 151, 185
"The High Country of the Mind" (Robert M. Pirsig) 137
Thick Data 80

tit for tat (Axelrod) 107
Tough Empathy xiii, 3, 41, 145, 146, 148, 149, 150, 155, 177, 182, 186, 190, 191
two-way empathy portal 95, 167

V

vetocracy (Dunkelman) 162